The ROCK & ROLL *Cookbook*

Dick and Sandy St. John
aka Dick and Dee Dee

with Pamela Des Barres

GPG

GENERAL
PUBLISHING
GROUP, INC

The publisher and authors wish to thank the following people for their contributions to the book: Hilary Bein, Diane Budy, Kevin Corcoran, Murray Fisher, Quendrith Johnson, Larry Klein, Margo Leavin Gallery, Sharon Lynn, Irene Robinson, Tony Seidl, John Valenzuela, Kurt Wahlner, Ron Wolfson and Mark Young.

Special thanks to Michael Ochs of the Michael Ochs Archives, Venice, California, for his kind contributions from his vast collection of Rock & Roll photographs—the greatest collection in the world.

Very special thanks to the artists, managers, agents, chefs and relatives for their generous contributions to this special project and for their genuine concern for their fellow music industry professionals.

The National Music Foundation:
Dick Clark, Chairman of the Board
Gloria Pennington, President and CEO
Founders: Joey Dee, Dr. Allen Haimes,
   Judith Haimes, Lois Lee
Jacque Veltman, Administrative Assistant
Call 1-800-USA-MUSIC or 310-459-5739
for more information

Library of Congress Cataloging-in-Publication Data:
St. John, Dick.
   The Rock & Roll cookbook: favorite recipes from the chart toppers, hit makers and legends of Rock & Roll / Dick and Sandy St. John, with Pamela Des Barres.
   Includes indexes.
   ISBN 1-881649-07-5 (pbk.) : $14.99
   1. Cookery. 2. Rock musicians. I. St John, Sandy. II. Des Barres. Pamela. III. Title.
TX714.S733   1993
641.5—dc20   93-25839
                                                        CIP

Publisher: W. Quay Hays
Managing Editor: Sarah Pirch
Assistant Editor: Colby Allerton
Cover collage: Susan Shankin
Copy Editors: Nancy McKinley and Paul Murphy
a daly design

Contents

To Jackie Wilson

Man, could he cook!

The National Music Foundation
MISSION STATEMENT

The National Music Foundation is a not-for-profit organization dedicated to American music and the people who bring it to us. Our mission is twofold:

1. To educate the public about American music in order to preserve our nation's musical heritage;

2. To provide for the retirement of professionals from the fields of music, radio and recording, with provisions made for those who can't afford to retire on their own.

We will fulfill this mission through The National Music Center.

The National Music Center's educational facilities will include an interactive museum, a performance center, a library and archive and a radio broadcast facility. All forms, styles and genres of American music will be represented, as will radio and the recording industry. Through scholarships, grants and mentor programs, the Center will encourage students to pursue studies of American music at all educational levels.

The Center will include a residence where professionals from music, radio and recording can retire among their peers.

We believe that American music, in its endless variety, is an important element in the national heritage of every citizen.

Introduction
"Hey Good Lookin', Watcha Got Cookin'?"

You're holding in your hands the world's greatest Rock & Roll cookbook. Every one of the recipes here is a number-one hit from a number-one star. As you look through this book, I think you'll meet some old friends. Their songs have become part of our lives over the years. You may never have met Little Eva or The Drifters, but I'll bet their songs have brought a smile to your face and an occasional tear to your eye. I know every time I hear "Under the Boardwalk," I think of hot summer days at the beach and the "hot dogs and french fries they sell."

Now I'd like you to ask yourself a question: Can you imagine your life without music?

Music accompanies our good times and helps us through the hard times. I just can't picture what life would be like without it. It's easy to forget that the musicians who sang for us can fall on hard times, too. Jackie Wilson inspired my good friend Joey Dee to establish The National Music Foundation. It is Joey's dream to provide a place for musicians so that those who have brought us so much joy will know that we'll be there for them when they need us. It's a dream I share wholeheartedly.

Dick and Sandy St. John (you know them better as Dick and Dee Dee—remember "The Mountain's High?") and Pamela Des Barres have put this wonderful book together to raise funds for The National Music Foundation. Proceeds from this cookbook will go to this important cause. So remember that as you "cook around the clock," you're returning a favor to some old friends.

DICK CLARK

Foreword

Rock & Roll has changed a lot since its beginning in the '50s. Those were the days of the 45 record, and to be a "Rock & Roll star" you had to have a hit single. Back then, the times were innocent—for $40 an enterprising sixteen-year-old could cut a demo and three months later might have a million selling hit record. Many of the pioneers you'll read about in this book actually started that way. But the flip side to this is the fact that in the '50s and '60s many recording artists didn't get paid properly. There are fond memories of nights on a bus in 1963, driving along with fifteen of the top recording artists in the world—and everyone laughing and singing "Mockingbird" or "Land Of A Thousand Dances." No one seemed to care that at the end of one of these grueling bus tours, they would go home with only enough money to buy a new set of stage clothes and hit the road again. As a result of this, too many of these beloved entertainers who were the roots of Rock & Roll have died penniless or live in poverty even though their records continue to be played around the world every day.

In June 1988, we had just returned home from a week on the road with a '60s Rock & Roll show. It was a week spent with old friends laughing and reminiscing about the old days. We hadn't been in the house more than fifteen minutes when the phone rang. It was Joey Dee—another voice from the past. But Joey wanted to talk about the future. That was the beginning of our involvement with what is now The National Music Foundation.

We've always felt that the music industry should have a home where singers, songwriters and musicians could retire if they were in need. The film industry takes care of its own with the Motion Picture Home, and it only makes sense for the music industry to do the same. That's why we decided to create this cookbook. It's been quite an experience talking to old friends we hadn't talked to in years, and finding that after talking only a few seconds it seemed that just a few days had passed since we'd last spoke. We all whistled while we worked, and sang and laughed and cheered as each recipe came in from all the good and caring people who contributed.

We thank Father/Mother God for bringing this idea into fruition, and dedicate this book to the future of The National Music Foundation, to the pioneers of Rock & Roll who have graduated from this school of life and to the loving memory of our mothers—Mrs. Howard (Idell) Houck and Irene Carroll Statum. Now get out there and rattle those pots and pans!
DICK AND SANDY ST. JOHN

Preface

To say that Rock & Roll has taken up a massive chunk of my life would be a sincere understatement. Everything I've ever done has had a song running through it. Dum-didla-dum-didla-doo-wop-bop-crash-bang-boom-rama-lama-dum-dum-dum-dum-de-doo-wah-ooh-yay-yay-yay-ye-aaaahhh!

My 45 player was truly my prized teen possession, and I would lay in my bedroom and swoon to Elvis and Dion, Bobby Rydell and Gene Pitney, sobbing over the unreachability of my idols. If somebody had told me that one day I would be working with Dick and Dee Dee, I would have said, "The mountain's high and the valley's so deep, can't get across to the other side...wo wo wo."

Not content to sit and swoon, I headed for the Sunset Strip in the '60s and made my teenage dreams come true by meeting, hanging out with and becoming one with my rock heroes. After writing a couple of books about my wacky life, I was called "Queen of the Groupies" on the Today Show, and I still don't know whether to blush all over or take a sweeping bow!

My heart still pounds for Rock & Roll, and working on this project for The National Music Foundation with Dick and Sandy St. John has been a triple thrill. Besides getting to sing soulful oldie hits with Dick while we hung on the phone with managers, publicists and superstars, I've seen firsthand just how caring and concerned all the rock guys and dolls really are. Most of them wrote their recipes out in longhand, including little personal notes, drawings and photos. Iggy Pop composed his own madcap bio for us, and Michael Hutchence from INXS described to me the glory of eating fresh langostino "with gallons of red wine" at a Paris café at midnight, while I scribbled it all down on a napkin! Peter Frampton was so concerned about the tastiness of his roasted potatoes that he called to see if I had personally tried out his recipe. "I know I spelled 'basted' wrong," he confessed gallantly.

What scary things did Alice Cooper throw into the blender to recover from a manic night in front of 20,000 ballistic fans? What kind of strange, fancy soup did Nirvana cook up? Would you believe it's full of fruit? I've always wondered what Ozzy Osbourne loves to eat with his rare roast beef, haven't you? Well dolls, you're about to find out.

PAMELA DES BARRES

Conversion Table for Weight Measurements (Approximate)

OUNCES TO GRAMS

Ounces	Grams	Ounces	Grams
1	28	4	113
1 ½	43	4 ½	128
2	57	5	142
2 ½	71	5 ½	156
3	85	6	170
3 ½	99		

Conversion Table for Volume Measurements

TEASPOONS TO MILLILITERS

tsp	ml
1/2	2.5
1	5.0
1 ½	7.5
2	10.0
2 ½	12.5
3	15.0

TEASPOONS TO TABLESPOONS

tsp	Tbsp
1	⅓
2	⅔
3	1
6	2
9	3

TABLESPOONS TO MILLILITERS

Tbsp	ml	Tbsp	ml
½	7.5	2 ½	37.5
1	15.0	3	45.0
1 ½	22.5	3 ½	52.5
2	30.0	4	60.0

QUARTS TO LITERS

quarts	liters	quarts	liters
1	1.0	3	3.0
1 ½	1.5	3 ½	3.5
2	2.0	4 (or	4.0
2 ½	2.5	1 gallon)	

OVEN TEMPERATURE CHART

Recipe Calls For:	Fahrenheit Degrees	Centigrade Degrees
Warm	200–225	93–107
Very Low	250–275	121–135
Low	300–325	149–163
Medium	350–375	177–191
High	400–425	204–218
Very High	450–475	232–246
Extremely High	500–525	260–274
Broil	600	316

Formula for converting from Fahrenheit to Centigrade:
Start with °F temperature,
Subtract 32,
Multiply by 5,
Divide by 9,
Result is °C temperature equivalent.

Formula for converting from Centigrade to Fahrenheit:
Start with °C temperature,
Multiply by 9,
Divide by 5,
Add 32,
Result is °F temperature equivalent.

ABBREVIATIONS FOR MEASURING UNITS

Unit Name	Symbol	Unit Name	Symbol
Centigrade, degree	°C	meter	m
centimeter	cm	milligram	mg
Fahrenheit, degree	°F	milliliter	ml
gram	g	ounce	oz
inch	in	pint, liquid	pt
kilogram	kg	pound	lb
liter	liter	quart, liquid	qt
		tablespoon	Tbsp
		teaspoon	tsp

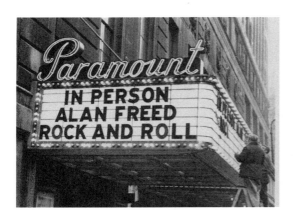

"Anyone who says Rock & Roll is a passing fad or a flash in the pan has rocks in his head, dad."
—Alan Freed
the legendary disc jockey who coined the term "Rock & Roll" and first brought the music and its artists to the attention of the American public

1

Appetizers

Taboulie My Way

Lotus Blossom Oriental Chicken Wings

**Turn Me Loose In The Kitchen And I'll Make
Stuffed Mushrooms**

South Street Grilled Cajun Shrimp And Crab Sticks

Gene's Jerky From "The Town Without Pity" Cafe

Paul Anka

Paul Anka has written some of the world's most widely recognized music. From "Put Your Head On My Shoulder" to "My Way" to the theme from the former *Tonight Show Starring Johnny Carson*, his songs have brought pleasure to millions of people.

Paul's first hit, "Diana," was recorded when he was just sixteen, and it began a string of popular singles that stretched from the '50s to the '80s. During that time, his songs have been recorded by everyone from Frank Sinatra to Elvis Presley to Sid Vicious. His songwriting collaborators have included Dionne Warwick, Richard Marx, Carole Bayer Sager and Michael Jackson.

Enough, you say, for one talented man's career? Wait—there's more. Paul lived in Italy between 1964 and 1966, and developed a special love for the country and its people. He has sold over two million records there and took top honors at the San Remo Song Festival. He has recorded more than ten albums in Italian, Spanish, German, French and Japanese, with the songs composed to fit the language and culture of each country.

Paul also has become interested in TV production and acting and he collects fine art and fine wines.

And finally—he makes a great taboulie!

"Taboulie is my favorite salad. There are many variations of the dish, but this is the one I grew up with. It's guaranteed to make all the women beautiful and all the men virile."

Taboulie My Way

3 bunches parsley
2 medium-ripe tomatoes
1/2 cup bulgur (cracked wheat—
   available at health food stores)
4 green onions
Juice of 1 fresh lemon (or to taste)
2 Tbsp pure olive oil (or to taste)
1 clove garlic, finely chopped
Salt and pepper

Wash parsley thoroughly. Throw away stems. Chop finely and place in bowl. Dice tomatoes and add to parsley. Soak bulgur in enough water to cover for 2 hours, then squeeze out water and mix with parsley and tomatoes. Dice green onion bulbs and part of the green tops. Add green onion and garlic to salad. Squeeze fresh lemon juice over salad. Add olive oil. Toss well with 2 spoons. Add salt and pepper to taste. Serve with pita bread quarters or romaine lettuce leaves.

The Blossoms
Fanita James

Fanita James is an original member of The Blossoms, one of the most famous "back-up" groups in the world. They provided background vocals for numerous recording artists including Dionne Warwick, The Righteous Brothers, Frank Sinatra, Jackie Wilson and Elvis Presley.

For over twenty years, Fanita, along with Jean King and Darlene Love, toured with Tom Jones, performing all over the world. She has many wonderful memories of those days on the road. Once while on stage, a "carried away" female fan stood up on her table at the back of the room. Because the tables were so close together she was able to literally "table hop" her way up to the stage before security guards could stop her. On her way there, the fan succeeded in removing her blouse and then her bra! The Blossoms, trying to continue with the show, could

not believe what was happening. Arriving on stage just seconds before the stage security team, the woman managed to get a kiss from Tom. He took her bra, mopped his brow and had the security guards lead her back to her seat to watch the rest of the show. Fanita also remembers that at the end of every tour, Tom would give each of The Blossoms a beautiful gift—always something made of gold.

In the early '60s, The Blossoms were the first female vocal group to win the Black Image Award and in the mid-'60s, they were featured on the TV show *Shindig*.

Prior to joining The Blossoms, Fanita was a member of Bob B. Soxx and the Blue Jeans, who had such memorable Phil Spector-produced hits as "Zip A Dee Doo Dah" and "Why Do Lovers Break Each Other's Hearts?".

Today, Fanita makes her home in Los Angeles and continues to perform. Her daughter and son are both college graduates.

Lotus Blossom Oriental Chicken Wings

Chicken wings

Recipe for sauce mix:
1 1/2 cups sugar
1 cup vinegar
1 cup ketchup
2 cloves garlic, diced
   (or garlic powder to taste)
4 Tbsp soy sauce

Mix all ingredients and pour mixture over chicken wings. Bake at 300° for two hours.

Fabian

An overnight singing sensation and a film star with over 30 films to his credit, Fabian was one of the biggest teenage Rock & Roll sensations of the late '50s. By the time he was eighteen, he had recorded eight albums and had earned gold records for the singles "Turn Me Loose" and "Tiger" and a gold album for *The Fabulous Fabian*.

In 1959, Fabian made his big screen debut in *Hound Dog Man*. Serious about his craft, he studied in New York for three years under Wynn Handman and in Hollywood with Charles Conrad and Sandy Meisner. His impressive acting credits include featured roles with John Wayne, James Stewart, Jack Palance and George Segal—not bad for a kid who was discovered at the age of fourteen sitting on the front steps of his home in Philadelphia!

Today, Fabian makes his home in Los Angeles and continues to perform in Fabian's Goodtime Rock & Roll Show, as well as with Frankie Avalon and Bobby Rydell as The Golden Boys. He is also a film and TV producer for Rattlesnake Productions.

In 1985, Fabian's Rock & Roll show was the first concert ever produced for pay-per-view television. The extravaganza was taped in front of 85,000 people in Baton Rouge, Louisiana, and later became a syndicated TV special as well as a PBS pledge-week special.

The years have definitely been kind to Fabian. No one would believe that on February 6, 1993, the Fabulous Fabian turned 50!

Turn Me Loose In The Kitchen And I'll Make Stuffed Mushrooms

2 lbs large, evenly sized mushrooms
1/2 cup grated Parmesan cheese
3/4 cup dry bread crumbs
1/2 cup onions, grated
2 cloves garlic, minced

3 Tbsp parsley, minced
1 tsp salt
1/2 tsp black pepper, freshly ground
1/2 tsp oregano
3/4 cup olive oil

Wash mushrooms, but do not peel. Remove and chop stems; mix with cheese, bread crumbs, onions, garlic, parsley, salt, pepper and oregano. Stuff the mushroom caps. Pour a little oil into a baking pan. Arrange mushrooms in it. Pour remaining oil over mushrooms, being sure to get a little on each one. Bake at 350° for 25 minutes. Serve as an antipasto, appetizer or vegetable. Serves 6 – 8.

The Orlons
Steve Caldwell and Marlena Davis Easley

The early '60s belonged to The Orlons. Not a day went by that you didn't hear "South Street" or "The Wah Watusi" or "Don't Hang Up."

In 1959, at Overbrook High School in Philadelphia, The Orlons began a most eventful and prosperous singing career. Len Barry, the lead singer with The Dovells, encouraged them to audition for Cameo Records. In 1961 they did just that, and signed a recording contract with Cameo-Parkway that resulted in a string of hits. During their very successful record-

ing career, they toured with The Dick Clark Tour, James Brown and Sam Cooke.

Today, sadly enough, Steve Caldwell is the only surviving member of The Orlons. Marlena Davis Easley passed away on February 27, 1993. She was preceded in death by Shirley Brickley and Rosetta Hightower. Before she passed away, Marlena and Dick St. John spoke several times on the telephone reminiscing about the old days on the road. Marlena was laughing as she recalled a particular Dick Clark tour when all the acts were backstage getting ready to board the bus to hit the road again. Someone happened to look out the window only to see that about seven people were removing all the suitcases and clothing bags from the bus and running off with them. Steve Caldwell took off after them and managed to retrieve some of the items, but many never did get their things back. It was one of those situations that was quite upsetting at the time and, only years later, could be laughed about.

Marlena was very excited about The National Music Foundation and submitted this recipe with Steve shortly before she died.

South Street Grilled Cajun Shrimp And Crab Sticks

Marinade:
1/2 cup vegetable or corn oil
1/4 cup red wine vinegar
1/4 cup soy sauce
1/4 cup steak sauce
1/4 cup Bullseye barbeque sauce
1/4 cup concentrated lemon juice
1/4 cup Worcestershire sauce

1/4 cup parsley flakes
1/2 tsp each of the following:
Paprika, seasoned salt or soul seasoning, onion powder, garlic powder, chili powder
1 Tbsp cayenne pepper
(or any kind of cajun seasoning)

Shrimp: Peel shrimp, except for tail, and de-vein.

Crab Sticks: Cut into even parts of 3 or 4 pieces.

Shrimp/Crab Sticks: Alternate shrimp and crab stick pieces (2 – 3 pieces of each is fine) onto skewers (if bamboo, soak 1 hour in water).

Put marinade ingredients into a large bowl and whisk until well blended. Add shrimp and crab-stick pieces and marinate for 30 minutes.

To Grill: Cook shrimp and crab sticks 6" above hot coals, 2 minutes per side or until pink in color. Dab on barbeque sauce and serve. Serves 8 – 10.

Gene Pitney

Behind every great performer lies a classic song. Gene Pitney began his career as a songwriter composing hit songs for other artists. He wrote "He's A Rebel" for the Crystals, "Rubber Ball" for Bobby Vee and "Hello Mary Lou" for Rick Nelson. Steve Lawrence, Tommy Edwards and Roy Orbison also recorded his material. Gene's song, "Today's Teardrops," was the B-side of Roy Orbison's monster hit, "Blue Angel."

Finding himself in heavy demand as a songwriter, Gene began to realize that he could sing his own songs. He wrote "I Wanna Love My Life Away" and decided to do the singing on the demo recording himself. The $30 demo was released as a single and became his first hit. Then the floodgates opened up to release a stream of hits: "Only Love Can Break A Heart," "Half Heaven, Half Heartache," "It Hurts To Be In Love," "Town Without Pity," "Twenty-Four Hours From Tulsa" and many others.

Today, Gene makes his home in Connecticut and is probably one of the most widely traveled artists in show business, regularly touring the world doing concerts, cabarets and TV appearances.

Gene's Jerky From The Town Without Pity Cafe

1 flank steak
1/2 cup soy sauce
1 clove garlic, mashed

1/4 tsp black pepper
2 Tbsp brown sugar

Slice steak in long strips, with the grain, with a 1/4" width. Mix sugar, garlic, black pepper and soy sauce. Stir until sugar has dissolved. Marinate meat at least 2 hours. Drain and place in shallow pan. Bake for 5 hours at 150°, or until meat is dry and cowboy chewy. Cut up into pieces and serve. Liberty Valance loved this stuff!

The Collector's Page

BILL HALEY

For information on how to order this Rock 'n' Roll/ Rhythm and Blues Commemorative Stamp, please see page 2.

2
Soups, Salads, Sauces and Side Dishes

Cinderella's Soup

The Maestro's Spanish Rice

So Good, So Good Creamed Corn

The Iceman's Make It Easy On Yourself Caesar Salad

All I Really Want To Do Is Make You Salade Niçoise

La Bamba Sopa De Mais (Corn Chowder)

Sea Cruise Crab Bisque

26 Smiles (Santa Catalina Seashell Salad)

English Roast Potatoes Come Alive

Surf City Clam Chowder

Louie Louie Salmon Chowder

Chuga-Chuga Yams

Smells Like Butternut Squash, Apple And Pear Soup

Ozzy's Yorkshire Pudding

Poetry In Motion Barbeque Sauce

The Night Has A Thousand Eyeland Dressing

Devil Or Angel Barbeque Sauce

Walk Don't Run For Macaroni Salad

The Beastie Boys
Mike Diamond

The Beastie Boys are fun-loving funky boys with fervent musical imaginations.

The band's debut album, *Licensed To Ill*, was the first rap record to top the U.S. charts, holding at number one for seven weeks. Produced by Rick Rubin for his new label, Def Jam, The Beasties gave the youth of America their own anthem, "(You Gotta) Fight For The Right (To Party)." Hard and heavy, raging with echo, it was the only viciously teenage rebel yell of the '80s to hit home around the world.

While they were on tour in the U.K. in late 1987, the tabloids invented lurid tales about The Beasties' supposedly anti-social behavior which, of course, helped to put *Licensed To Ill* into the British Top 10.

The Beasties' second album, *Paul's Boutique*, came out in 1989, and the most recent, *Check Your Head*, was recorded throughout 1991. As ever, there's a smorgasbord of references to the cuisine scene. This band is cursed and blessed with a junk rap diet and a snack-food vocabulary. "It's finger lickin' good," yell Adrock, MCA and Mike D.

"We recorded it live as a four-piece band because we wanted this s—- to be fat in both sound and attitude," says Mike D. "We went for a whole nine of fatness and I think we tipped the scales."

Through the years, The Beasties have branched out creatively. In 1989, Adam Horovitz (Adrock) starred in the film *Lost Angels*, and lately the boys have been marketing their own line of t-shirts and clothing under the X-Large label.

"On our last European tour, we had a great caterer who called herself Cinderella and this is really her recipe."
—Mike Diamond, 1993

Cinderella's Soup

2 Tbsp butter
4 large potatoes, peeled and thinly sliced
3 large or 5 small leeks, cleaned and
   chopped
1 white onion, chopped

3 cups vegetable stock
1 cup heavy cream
Salt and pepper
Chopped chives

In a 14"–18" sauté pan, sauté butter, onions and leeks until soft. Add potatoes and cover with vegetable stock. Simmer covered, stirring occasionally until potatoes are soft. Add salt and pepper to taste. Blend mixture in smallish batches in blender or food processor, alternately adding cream to the blender. Blend until smooth. If soup is too thick, add more stock and cream. Serve topped with chopped chives.

The Brooklyn Bridge
Johnny Maestro

The story of Johnny Maestro and The Brooklyn Bridge is one that spans virtually the entire rock era. It begins with The Crests in the latter half of the '50s, when Johnny began his career with the Manhattan-based group. Their first records generated some regional response, but the breakthrough of "Sixteen Candles" was what brought them national recognition. A string of hits followed, including "Trouble In Paradise," "Step By Step" and "The Angels Listened In." By the time the group disbanded in 1962, the record-buying public had developed a strong awareness of, and a great admiration for, the very special vocal abilities of Johnny Maestro.

As the music scene changed with the "British Invasion" of the early '60s, Johnny began working with The Del-Satins, a local New York vocal group. They did studio work with several artists and were most notably the background vocalists on all of Dion's solo efforts. While working the local club scene, Johnny and The Del-Satins met up with a seven-piece band called The Rhythm Method. The two bands were so impressed with each other that they decided to merge. Thus, The Brooklyn Bridge was formed.

The Brooklyn Bridge once again brought national attention to the voice of Johnny Maestro. His powerful performance of Jim Webb's "The Worst That Could Happen" led to a gold record for the group. Other hits followed, and by 1972 The Brooklyn Bridge had sold over ten million records, establishing Johnny Maestro as one of the great vocal talents of his era.

Today, The Brooklyn Bridge still performs to sold-out shows at major clubs and concert halls nationwide, and they're better than ever!

The Maestro's Spanish Rice

1/4 cup Goya olive oil
1 1/2 cans chicken broth
2 cups Carolina long grain rice
1 lb sweet sausage, casing removed
1 small jar capers

1 small jar green olives with pimento
1 small can tomato paste
1/2 green pepper
1 small onion, diced
1 can pink kidney beans (optional)

In a large cast-iron Dutch oven, mix oil, green pepper, onion and sausage. Over medium flame, cook sausage breaking it up with long fork (2 prong). While mixture is cooking, wash rice in warm water and drain. Go back to sausage and add tomato paste. Mix well with all ingredients. Add rice and mix well again; add broth slowly (the broth should just about be covering the rice). Add salt and pepper to taste. Cook on high flame until most of broth is absorbed. Cover, lower flame and cook 20 minutes. Uncover rice, mix with 2 prong fork. Add capers, olives and beans, then cover and cook an additional 15 minutes. Before serving, mix again with fork. Can be served with chicken, pork or steak.

James Brown

Mr. Dynamite. The hardest working man in show business. The Godfather of Soul. James surpassed living-legend status decades ago. Though his roots lie in gospel, his funk/R & B/soul magic continues to provide inspiration for many rockers today—from Prince to the Stones to Ice Cube.

The Godfather of Soul dropped out of school in the seventh grade and started educating himself in music, building on the gospel roots he discovered at church.

By the age of fifteen, he formed his own group, singing and dancing in the street to help support his family. At twenty, he joined a group with legendary gospel singer Bobby Byrd, and they were quick to advance to national acclaim as The Famous Flames.

The Flames brought the R & B scene to life in the Southeast, igniting sparks wherever they set up. James used his magic to break the boundaries of racial segregation, and both blacks and whites became engrossed in a sound once considered strictly "black music."

In 1956, he recorded "Please Please Please," which reached number six on the R & B charts. Since then, James has recorded 74 top R & B hits and has sold over 50 million records. With the exception of Elvis Presley, James has had more charting pop singles than any other artist in history. He's penned such inspirational and funk-filled classics as "Cold Sweat," "Say It Loud, I'm Black And I'm Proud" and "Papa's Got A Brand New Bag."

In 1992, as a result of his influential steps in music and a lifetime devoted to equality, James Brown was honored with the American Music Awards' Award Of Merit, as well as the National Academy of Recording Arts and Sciences Lifetime Achievement Award.

The title of his newest (79th) recording, *Universal James*, pretty much sums up his appeal.

So Good, So Good Creamed Corn

Corn on the cob
1 tsp butter
1 pinch flour
1 dash salt
1/2 tsp sugar
A little half and half or milk
Bacon drippings

Boil fresh corn on the cob. Cut corn from cob. Mix remaining ingredients with corn. Pour mixture into skillet with bacon drippings. Simmer slowly. Stir constantly until thick.

Jerry Butler

Three-time Grammy nominee Jerry "The Ice Man" Butler has enjoyed a long career that began in 1958 when he and Curtis Mayfield formed an R & B group in Chicago called The Roosters. That same year, the eighteen-year-old Jerry wrote a song called "For Your Precious Love" which launched Jerry Butler and The Impressions. He went on to have a string of hits including "He Will Break Your Heart," "Moon River" and "Make It Easy On Yourself."

During his career, Jerry has made appearances on *The Tonight Show Starring Johnny Carson*, *The Ed Sullivan Show*, *CBS Sunday Morning* and *The Today Show*. He has hosted and appeared in a number of other TV programs including the *Soul Show* for PBS and *Martin The Emancipator*—a tribute to Dr. Martin Luther King, Jr.

Jerry was inducted into the Rock & Roll Hall of Fame in 1991, but, at this point in his life, music is only one of two careers. Monday through Friday he can be found in the Cook County Commissioner's Office in Chicago, where he serves as Commissioner of the second largest county in the United States with over five million constituents.

Jerry and Annette, his wife of 33 years, have twin sons.

The Ice Man's Make It Easy On Yourself Caesar Salad

1 large head romaine lettuce
3 large cloves garlic, crushed
6 strips anchovies
4 Tbsp olive oil
4 Tbsp tarragon vinegar
1 Tbsp lime juice
Worcestershire sauce, dash
Tabasco sauce, dash
1 egg, coddled or raw
Salt
Parmesan cheese (optional)

Wash and break lettuce by hand into bite-sized pieces and chill. In a wooden salad bowl, crush garlic and anchovies with a touch of salt to make a paste. Add olive oil, tarragon vinegar, lime juice, Worcestershire and Tabasco. Stir until thoroughly mixed. Add chilled romaine and egg, mixing well so that dressing and egg saturate the lettuce. Sprinkle with Parmesan cheese and serve on chilled plate.

Cher

The first record on which Cher ever sang was "Be My Baby" for legendary producer Phil Spector. After meeting Sonny Bono in the early '60s while he was working for Phil, the two teamed as Caesar and Cleo before marrying in 1964 and becoming Sonny and Cher. For their debut single, they borrowed $168 and recorded "Baby Don't Go" and followed with "I Got You Babe," which sold more than three million records. The hits kept coming: "All I Really Want To Do," "Bang Bang," "The Beat Goes On" and on and on.

From 1965 to 1979, Cher—as half of Sonny and Cher and as a solo performer—enjoyed four number-one hits, twelve Top 10 and twenty-two Top 40 singles—eleven gold and three platinum. There was also success in Las Vegas, and in the summer of 1971, the premiere of the landmark *The Sonny And Cher Comedy Hour*. This popular series ended after four seasons, and the marriage after twelve.

Cher then set her sights on becoming an actress, winning a Golden Globe nomination for Best Supporting Actress in *Come Back To The Five and Dime, Jimmy Dean, Jimmy Dean* in the same role she played on Broadway. She followed with an Oscar nomination for Best Supporting Actress in *Silkwood*, received much critical acclaim for her performance in *Mask* and, in 1987, finally won a Best Actress Academy Award for her role in *Moonstruck*.

Also in 1987, she returned to a recording career on Geffen Records. Cher went gold with two hits, "I Found Someone" and "We All Sleep Alone." The follow-up, 1989's *Heart Of Stone*, went double platinum and spawned the gold single, "If I Could Turn Back Time." Says Cher, "If I had not come back to a music career, I would have missed doing this album. That would have been a real disappointment in my life. But you can either swim or die at points in your career. I swam. I'm a gutsy kind of gal."

All I Really Want To Do Is Make You Salade Niçoise

1 head romaine lettuce, cut and washed

1 cup haricot verts (French green beans), trimmed and blanched

1 red tomato, cored and sliced

1 yellow tomato, cored and sliced

1 cup Kalamata olives, pitted and sliced thin

4 hard-boiled eggs, quartered

4 Ahi tuna steaks (5–6 oz each)

8 red new potatoes, cooked, sliced 1/4" thick

1 bunch chives, snipped

1/2 red onion, minced

Fresh ground pepper

Arrange sliced potatoes around edge of plate. Sprinkle with chopped chives and minced red onion. Mound 1–1 1/2 cups lettuce mixed with tomatoes, green beans and olives in middle of plate. Brush fresh tuna with mixture of olive oil, black peppers and herbs. Grill to desired doneness. Cut into 4 slices. Place over lettuce mound. Drizzle dressing over entire salad. Garnish with egg quarters. Fresh ground pepper all over.

Dressing:

1/2 cup virgin olive oil

1/2 cup balsamic vinegar

Lemon juice/white wine vinegar (to taste)

1/4 cup cold chicken broth, canned

2 Tbsp capers

3 Tbsp anchovies, chopped

Salt and white pepper

Fresh thyme

1/4 cup Kalamata olives, pitted and chopped

Dijon mustard (optional)

Mix all ingredients together, except olive oil. Slowly whisk in olive oil until fully incorporated. Season to taste. Some

Dijon mustard can be added for an extra zing! Drizzle over salad.

Dick Clark

The National Music Foundation's Chairman of the Board, Dick Clark, entered the music business more than four decades ago. At age seventeen, he began announcing news, weather and station breaks at WRUN Radio in Utica, New York. After graduating from Syracuse University, he served as WKTV-TV's news anchor, also in Utica. In 1952, he moved to Philadelphia to work for WFIL radio and television where, in four years, he became the host of the station's local TV show *Bandstand*. Twelve months later, Dick convinced the ABC network to broadcast the show nationwide, and *American Bandstand* soon became the country's highest-rated daytime show. Generations of music fans watched *Bandstand* to see and hear the latest developments in Rock & Roll music. For thousands of performers, the show provided the first national exposure of their careers. *Bandstand* was recognized by the industry with several Emmy Awards, including Best Daytime Show, Best Direction, Best Editing and Program Achievement.

Today, Dick is the Chairman and Chief Executive Officer of the production company that bears his name. He took the Burbank-based company public in January 1987, and continues to develop and produce scores of TV series, movies and specials. One of Dick's specialties is the production of a major TV event, *The American Music Awards*, which first aired in 1974. Every year, he generously donates the net proceeds from the AMA ticket sales to The National Music Foundation.

Dick is very interested in musical history and the preservation of the artifacts of pop. His media archives include one of the world's largest music libraries on video, vintage kinescopes and films and a huge collection of Rock & Roll memorabilia, all of which are stored in climate-controlled vaults. Dick has also moved into the restaurant business with The American Bandstand Grill in Kansas City, which features dining and dancing against a backdrop of *American Bandstand* memorabilia.

LaBamba Sopa De Mais (Corn Chowder)

1 can (10 1/2 oz) Green Giant Mexicorn
1 cup frozen corn
1 cup onion, chopped
1 cup celery, chopped
4 cups skim milk
1 jar Progresso Roasted Peppers
   (drain oil and chop the peppers)
Celery Seed
Cayenne Pepper

Paprika
Garlic Powder
Salt
Coarse black pepper
Onion Powder
Marjoram
Beau Monde
2 Tbsp margarine

Place milk, frozen corn, canned Mexicorn and roasted peppers in large saucepan. Add spices to taste. IMPORTANT: the amounts of cayenne, black pepper and paprika used will determine how spicy the chowder becomes.

Sauté chopped onions and chopped celery in another frying pan, using margarine. Add to mixture. Simmer for 10–15 minutes. Let stand for 1–2 hours. Re-heat and serve.

Frankie Ford

Frankie Ford grew up in Louisiana and continues to live there in a town called Gretna just a few miles outside of New Orleans. Frankie owned a popular restaurant for many years in Gretna at which he often performed. He is a master of the keyboard and an incredibly funny comedian, as well as being the man behind the smash "Sea Cruise."

In 1959, Huey "Piano" Smith wrote the classic song and brought it to Frankie in hopes that he would record it. Frankie, knowing a monster hit when he heard it, didn't hesitate. By summer, everyone who listened to Rock & Roll was singing along to "Sea Cruise" with Frankie. The song was so recognizable that it recently was used to advertise Diet Coke and Sprite. Rock & Roll fans everywhere rent *American Hot Wax* or *My American Cousin* just to watch Frankie perform "Sea Cruise." Frankie continues to perform his wonderful hit "Sea Cruise" all over the world.

In his spare time (which is a rarity), Frankie loves to cook. He's an innovative chef, and when we've had the pleasure of doing shows with him, he's shared many wonderful secret recipes with us.

Sea Cruise Crab Bisque

1/2 cup celery, chopped
1/2 cup onion, chopped
1 Tbsp butter
1 can cream of chicken soup
1 can cream of mushroom soup

1 can cream of celery soup
3 soup cans milk
2 cans (10 3/4 oz each) crabmeat
Salt and pepper

Sauté celery and onions in butter until celery is soft and onions are transparent but not brown. Add the soups, milk and crabmeat. Simmer on low for 15–20 minutes. Do not boil. Add salt and pepper to taste. (Best made the day before serving. Refrigerate and gently heat before serving.)

The Four Preps
Bruce Belland

The Four Preps first catapulted into national prominence as teenage recording artists in 1958 when they released "26 Miles" on Capitol Records. Bruce Belland, Glen Larson, Ed Cobb and Marv Ingram met while attending Hollywood High School. Bruce came up with the idea to form The Four Preps and wrote "26 Miles" and the group was on its way! They continued their successful recording career with such hits as "Big Man," "Lazy Summer Night," "Down By The Station" and a string of others. In '62, '63 and '64, they were honored by *Billboard* magazine as the nation's number-one concert attraction. They have shared stages around the world with such stars as George Burns, Frank Sinatra, Bing Crosby, Louie Armstrong and Sammy Davis, Jr.

Several years ago, Bruce decided to take the advice of his longtime friend Dick Clark and re-formed The Four Preps as a vocal supergroup, featuring the original lead singers from three of the music world's most successful recording groups: The Four Preps (Bruce), The Diamonds and The Association. With accumulated record sales in excess of 100 million units, these four unique performers have established themselves as one of the country's most sought-after corporate, convention and concert acts, with engagements booked around the world as much as two years in advance.

Bruce makes his home in Encino, California, and in addition to performing is engaged in what he calls "the most satisfying and challenging experience of my life"—public speaking. His specialty is communicating his unique experiences and insights on the subject he knows best—recycling yourself in tough times!

26 Smiles
(Santa Catalina Seashell Salad)

1 lb medium macaroni shells
1 lb Bay shrimp, cleaned
1 cup celery, finely chopped
1 cup green onion, finely chopped
1 cup sweet pickle relish
Mayonnaise
2 Tbsp dill weed
1/2 cup olive oil
Salt and pepper

Cook macaroni shells in boiling water seasoned with dill weed and olive oil. When shells are cooked, drain and set aside to cool. When shells are cool, mix in celery, onion and sweet pickle relish. Add shrimp. Mix with mayonnaise to moisten. Add salt and pepper to taste. Refrigerate several hours before serving.

Peter Frampton

Peter Frampton has been in love with the guitar since he was an eight-year-old kid growing up in England when he first saw Buddy Holly, The Everly Brothers and Hank Marvin, the lead guitarist with The Shadows.

Peter began his career at age sixteen with The Herd, a teen-oriented British pop band, and soon the British music press dubbed him "The Face Of 1968." Soon after, he teamed up with Steve Marriott of The Small Faces to form Humble Pie, and stayed with the band through three albums, leaving when it became clear that Humble Pie was evolving into a strictly hard rock band. Peter preferred a wider musical range, and in 1972 he decided to try his luck as a solo artist.

Criss-crossing the country with his first four albums, he gradually built up his audience. Then, in January 1976, Peter recorded *Frampton Comes Alive!*, which became *Billboard*'s number-one album of 1976. Frampton was also the biggest concert draw of the hotly competitive Bicentennial summer, selling nearly two million concert tickets!

Frampton Comes Alive! remains the best-selling live album in history, and A & M Records has just released *Shine On—A Collection*, a two-decade retrospective of Peter's solo career.

Cameron Crowe concluded his introductory essay for *Shine On* by noting, "Very simply, Frampton stayed true to his music, his songs and his guitar. He plays them with the unfaded love of someone whose hobby became a lifelong passion. For Peter Frampton, music is a labor of love. Along the way, he made history."

English Roast Potatoes Come Alive

Potatoes
3 Tbsp cooking oil
Butter or margarine

Salt and pepper
Seasoning of your choice

Preheat the oven to 400°. Peel and cut all the potatoes to about the same size. Usually you can cut 1 large potato into 3 potential "roast potatoes!" Then put them in boiling water for 5 minutes. As they are boiling, you have just enough time to listen to your favorite Led Zeppelin track. You need a baking pan big enough to fit all your slightly boiled potatoes comfortably. I find that during the guitar solo is the best time to put the cooking oil into the pan. Now they have finished boiling, so put them into the pan and put butter or margarine on them. Sprinkle with salt and pepper, and a seasoning of your choice would be good at this time. Place the pan in the oven and cook. You should periodically baste the potatoes and they will turn a nice golden brown. I can't remember how long you keep them in the oven but keep basting and keep checking and you can't go wrong!

Jan and Dean
Jan Berry

Jan Berry was the driving force behind the team when they began back in 1958. It was Jan who said, "We can have a hit," like other teen stars of that era. He had two tape recorders but no microphone. That didn't stop Jan. He "borrowed" the assembly microphone from his high school auditorium and was in business. From early in the duo's career to their peak at the top of the charts, Jan was always coming up with new ideas.

After a few hits in the early '60s, Jan and Dean were doing some "hops" with The Beach Boys, performing live with them on a number of occasions. So it seemed natural on their next album to do a Jan and Dean version of "Surfin'" and "Surfin' Safari." Just maybe they could "con" the Beach Boys into cutting the instrumental tracks and maybe even "help out" on some of the vocals. It worked. After the session, Brian Wilson said he had a song that wasn't completed, but if they wanted to finish it they could record it. He played the intro to "Surf City" on the piano. In 1963, it was number one in the nation and Top 10 in nearly every other country in the world, becoming the biggest hit of Jan and Dean's long and successful career.

In April 1966, Jan was involved in a tragic automobile accident. The doctors told his family that he would never be a fully functioning person again. That was many years ago, however, and Jan's tremendous spirit proved them wrong. He and wife Gertie live in Brentwood, California, and he continues to sing and travel. He even drives his own car again.

The group's career successes keep coming. In 1980, the City of Los Angeles honored the duo by declaring a Jan and Dean Day, and in 1986, Jan and Dean became the first Rock & Roll act to tour the People's Republic of China.

Surf City Clam Chowder

1 can (10 oz) cream of potato soup
1 cup milk
1/8 tsp black pepper, freshly ground
6 or 10 oz can baby clams (rinse well)
1 can (16 oz) whole potatoes,
   cut into small pieces
1/2 cup celery, sliced
1/4 cup red onions, chopped

Mix all ingredients in a pot. Bring to a boil, then decrease heat to simmer. Warm for about 5 minutes. Serves 2–3 hearty servings or 4–6 smaller servings.

The Kingsmen
Dick Peterson

"Louie, Louie" was the hit that made The Kingsmen infamous. In 1963, they were playing local teenage nightclubs and high school proms in their hometown of Portland, Oregon. A local deejay liked what he heard and asked the group to make a demo. The recording process took about one hour and cost approximately $40. The record was titled "Louie, Louie," and The Kingsmen were an overnight sensation. By the end of the year they received a gold record at a party in New York City, and we were there to celebrate with them. Since its first release, this legendary hit has sold over twenty million records. "Louie, Louie" has been the overwhelming favorite theme song of fraternities, sororities and high schools throughout the world. The Kingsmen's "Louie, Louie" almost became a hit all over again when it was featured in the popular movie, *Animal House*.

The band literally grew up together on the road during a five-year tour, developing a real closeness between the three remaining original members: Dick Peterson, Mike Mitchell and Barry Curtis. That bond is still apparent to audiences who watch them perform today, over 25 years later.

Currently, in addition to performing all around the country, The Kingsmen have done TV commercials for California Cooler and Purina Chex Party Mix. But all this infamy hasn't gone to their heads: They're still the hometown boys of Portland, Oregon.

Louie, Louie Salmon Chowder

1 cup salmon, cooked, flaked, fresh or canned
1/2 cup celery, chopped
1/2 cup onion, chopped
1/2 cup green pepper, chopped (optional)
1 clove garlic, minced
3 Tbsp butter
1 cup potatoes, diced

1 cup carrot, shredded
2 cups chicken broth
1 1/2 tsp salt
1/2 tsp pepper
1/2 tsp dill weed
1 can (17 oz) cream-style corn
1 can (13 oz) evaporated milk or cream

Sauté celery, onion, pepper and garlic in butter until onion is translucent. Add potatoes, carrots, chicken broth and seasonings. Simmer for 20 minutes and add corn, salmon and evaporated milk or cream. Heat thoroughly and serve. Serves 4–6.

Little Eva

Born in Belhaven, North Carolina, Eva Harris ("Little Eva") couldn't decide whether to be a nurse or a singer. She loved to sing more than anything in the world and sang whenever and wherever she could, mostly in school productions and in the church choir. She didn't know how her dream would ever come true. Then she answered what turned out to be a miraculous ad for a babysitter/housekeeper!

When Eva went to work for songwriters Carole King and Gerry Goffin as their "domestic assistant," she had no idea that she would wind up having a smash hit record. But that's what happened—almost like a fairy tale come true. Carole and Gerry had written a song called "The Loco-Motion" that Eva liked to sing while working around the house—and, well, the rest is history! It was number one by the end of the summer of 1962 and, needless to say, changed Eva's life.

Eva still makes her home in North Carolina in the town of Kingston. She has just recently started performing again, and her engagements included a recent appearance at the Greek Theatre in Los Angeles where she brought the house down. She loves being back on the concert circuit and not long ago met Dee Dee Sharp

for the first time. Since meeting, they've become great friends and can't believe that they had never met before now, 30 years after their careers began.

We've still only "met" Eva by telephone, but she is an exceptionally nice person, and we look forward to working with her one day soon.

LITTLE EVA

Chuga-Chuga Yams

3 lbs yams
1 Tbsp nutmeg
1 Tbsp cinnamon
Sugar

Orange peel
1 stick butter or margarine
1 Tbsp vanilla extract

Cut yams into pieces and put into baking pan. Sprinkle with the other ingredients. Cover with water, and season to your own taste. Bake at 350° until soft.

Nirvana
Kurt Cobain

"Punk is musical freedom," says Nirvana's guitarist/singer Kurt Cobain. "It's saying, doing and playing what you want. In Webster's terms, 'nirvana' means freedom from pain, suffering and the external world, and that's pretty close to my definition of punk rock."

In the beginning, Nirvana played underground punk shows in Tacoma, Washington, quickly gaining an audience, critical acclaim and a record deal with Seattle-based Sub Pop, which released Nirvana's debut album, 1989's *Bleach*. In 1990, Nirvana exited Sub Pop for the more substantial DGC Records. "Being on a major label has had no effect on *Nevermind*," insists Cobain about their massive-selling, massively important second album, "except that it was nice to have the freedom to take more time. We recorded *Bleach* in six days. We did this one in three weeks."

The youth of America went bonkers over Nirvana and the "Seattle Sound." *Nevermind* was full of hit singles, and "Smells Like Teen Spirit" became an anthem that has been parodied by Weird Al Yankovic in an hilariously accurate rendition.

About "Teen Spirit," Cobain says, "My generation's apathy. I'm disgusted with it. I'm disgusted with my own apathy too, for being spineless and not always standing up against racism, sexism and all those other -isms the counterculture has been whining about for years."

"What people don't realize is that the so-called Seattle Grunge scene grew out of several close-knit gourmet supper clubs—we would only pick up guitars to pass the time while our dishes were simmering, baking, boiling, etc."

– Kurt Cobain, 1993

Smells Like Butternut Squash, Apple And Pear Soup

3 Tbsp butter
10 white onions, chopped
2 lbs butternut squash,
    peeled and chopped
2 apples, peeled, cored and quartered
1 Asian pear
2 qts vegetable stock

1/4 tsp tarragon
1/2 cup dry vermouth
1 cup heavy cream
Salt, black pepper and white pepper
Garnish:
5 tsp fresh chives, chopped
5 cups sour cream

Melt butter in a deep skillet over a low flame. Sauté the onions, squash, apples and pear in the butter until tender. Add the vegetable stock, tarragon, salt and white pepper to your liking. Bring the whole concoction to a boil then cover and simmer over a low flame until the squash and apples are fully cooked (approximately 5 minutes). Remove from heat and purée in a food processor until creamy. Then, stir in the cream and the vermouth. Season to taste with salt and pepper. Serve hot with a dollop of sour cream and a sprinkle of chives.

Ozzy Osbourne

Ozzy Osbourne—singer, songwriter, performer extraordinaire, legend and all-around madman—has dangled on Rock & Roll's jagged precipice for two-and-a-half decades.

In Birmingham, England, back in 1968, he joined schoolmates and neighbors to form a group called Earth, which the following year became Black Sabbath. In 1970, they released their first self-titled album. With six more albums featuring Ozzy as its lead singer, Black Sabbath became the unchallenged king of heavy metal in the '70s. In 1979, Ozzy left to pursue a solo career with his new band, The Blizzard of Ozz. Their first album stayed on the U.S. charts for two years.

Through each of his many studio efforts, all platinum-plus million sellers, Ozzy the myth, with his outrageous sense of Rock & Roll drama, has obscured Ozzy the artist, whose emotional song-writing and presentation explains better than anything else the enormous appeal of Ozzy the rock icon. Perhaps this is because he's never shied away from the extremes—skull-crushing rock to romantic ballads, excessive abuse to vocal sobriety—and in the process has assured his place in the annals of Rock & Roll.

Ozzy's fame is worldwide. Even when he performed at a rock festival in Moscow's Lenin Stadium in 1989, on a bill with Bon Jovi and Mötley Crüe, he was greeted by fans as the festival's true hero holding flying banners proclaiming, "Ozzy is God."

Time and again, Ozzy has insisted he's not a spokesman or symbol for anyone or anything, just a Rock & Roller committed to the emotion of his music. He currently lives in England and Los Angeles with his wife, Sharon, and their three children.

Ozzy's Yorkshire Pudding

3 oz flour
1 egg
3 fl oz milk

2 fl oz water
Salt and freshly milled pepper
2 Tbsp beef dripping

To make the batter, sift flour into a bowl, make a hole in the center, break an egg into it and beat it while incorporating the flour, milk, water and seasoning. Heat oven to high (450– 500°). Put 2–3 tsp of oil in each cup of a metal muffin tin. Heat the tin with oil until very, very hot. When hot, pour batter into tins, filling each to about 3/4 full (the yorkies grow, so leave some room). Place in hot oven and bake 10–15 minutes. Do not open the oven door until they are done, as yorkshires will flop. Serve with roast beef or chicken, vegetables and lots of mashed potatoes and gravy for an authentic English lunch.

Johnny Tillotson

Johnny was born in Jacksonville, Florida, and by the age of nine he knew he wanted to be a singer. When his parents realized his genuine interest in music, they bought him a guitar. By the time he started high school, he had already organized his own band and was working up and down the entire state of Florida.

When Johnny started college at the University of Florida, he also had his own local TV show. For two years he commuted between the university campus and the TV studio exchanging the roles of student and emcee/performer. During this time, he also began writing songs. In 1957, he entered a songwriting contest sponsored by Pet Milk and was chosen as one of the six national winners to be sent to Nashville to compete in the finals. Although Johnny didn't win first place, he did impress many influential people in the audience and was brought to the attention of Archie Bleyer, president of Cadence Records, who was in town doing a recording session with The Everly Brothers. Archie released three records on Cadence before Johnny broke through with his number-one hit, "Poetry In Motion." This record was a hit not only in the United States but also the world over and established Johnny as an international recording artist. This acclaim was followed by a total of eighteen chart records including "It Keeps Right On A Hurtin'," "Talk Back Trem-blin' Lips" and "Heartaches By The Number," which received a 1965 Grammy nomination for Best Male Vocal Performance.

Today, Johnny lives with his wife Nancy in Encino, California, and performs internationally in nightclubs, at fair dates and in concert.

Poetry In Motion Barbeque Sauce

1 bottle (14 oz) ketchup
1/2 cup water
1/2 cup colored vinegar
2 Tbsp sugar

1 Tbsp salt
1 Tbsp Worcestershire sauce
1 Tbsp coarse black pepper

Mix together and bring to a boil. Stir often—tends to stick. Makes 3 cups. Great for chicken or ribs. It's true "Poetry in Motion."

Bobby Vee

On February 3, 1959, a light plane carrying Buddy Holly, Richie Valens, The Big Bopper and twenty-year-old pilot Roger Peterson crashed in a snow-covered Iowa field, killing everyone on board. Only minutes earlier they had finished their performance at the Surf Ballroom in Clearlake, Iowa, and had rushed to the airport in nearby Mason City to catch the charter plane that was to bring them to their next engagement in Moorhead, Minnesota. News of the tragedy traveled fast. People at the local radio station in Moorhead—like everyone—were in a state of shock. The rest of the tour had arrived from Clearlake by bus after a cold and snowy all-night drive. A decision was made to continue on with the show and the promoters asked for local talent to help fill in on that sad night. As the curtain came up that evening, a new voice was introduced to the world: a fifteen-year-old voice who knew all the words to all the songs—Bobby Vee.

In the following 30 years, Bobby would go on to chart 38 songs in the *Billboard* Top 100 with six gold singles—"Devil Or Angel," "Rubber Ball," "Take Good Care Of My Baby," "Run To Him," "The Night Has A Thousand Eyes" and "Come Back When You Grow Up"—fourteen Top 40 hits and two gold albums.

Today Bobby lives with his family in St. Cloud, Minnesota. He continues to tour regularly and was part of the 1988 "Tour from Hell" with Dick and Dee Dee, Brian Hyland, Tommy Roe and Dickey Lee. It was one of those tours that was just like the "good ol' days," and we all still laugh about it.

The Night Has A Thousand Eyeland Dressing

1 cup mayonnaise
1 Tbsp ketchup
2 hard-boiled eggs, chopped
1 cup sour cream

A few little green onions, finely chopped
1 Tbsp fresh lemon juice

Mix thoroughly.

Devil Or Angel Barbeque Sauce

2 tsp mustard
2 cups ketchup
2 tsp salt
2 tsp pepper
3 tsp garlic salt
1/8 bottle (2 oz) vinegar
1/2 bottle (5 oz) A-1 Steak Sauce
1/2 bottle (5 oz) Heinz 57 Sauce
1/2 box brown sugar

Heat and stir in saucepan (on the grill, of course!). For chicken, add 1/2 cup of salad oil to the above ingredients.

The Ventures
Mel Taylor

One of the best-selling and most influential instrumental groups in the history of Rock & Roll is without a doubt The Ventures. Etched permanently in the annals of rock music are their classic hits "Walk Don't Run," "Perfidia," "Slaughter On 10th Avenue," "Hawaii Five-O," "Pipeline," "Wipeout" and many others.

The Ventures have not only sold millions of albums of contemporary guitar music, but have also marketed millions of albums teaching other people to play the instrument. In fact, their "Play Guitar With The Ventures" series features the only instruction albums ever to appear on the national *Billboard* charts.

The group was formed in 1959 by Don Wilson and Bob Bogle, who met on a construction job in Seattle. They started taking guitar lessons together and before long were playing in clubs at night while still working their day jobs. They recorded "Walk Don't Run," which local Seattle radio stations soon started to play. The record attracted the attention of Doltan Records, a subsidiary of Liberty Records, who signed the group. That was the beginning of a long and successful career.

Now in their fourth decade, The Ventures have been the best-selling rock-pop instrumental group in the world. In Japan, where their popularity can be compared to that of the Beatles at the height of Beatlemania, they are national heroes. The Ventures continue to tour all over the world bringing their music to fans—old and new. As drummer Mel Taylor points out, "Our audience is filled with people from 5 to 50."

Walk Don't Run For Macaroni Salad

1 lb macaroni
   (elbow, fusilli or small shells)
1 lb canned baby peas
1 lb lean bacon

1 cup mayonnaise
Salt and pepper
Parsley
Hard-boiled egg

Fry bacon until crisp. Drain on paper towels. When cool, crumble into 1/2" pieces. Cook macaroni according to package directions (*al dente*—do NOT overcook). Rinse and drain well and allow to cool. Pour macaroni into large bowl and add crumbled bacon. Add mayonnaise and mix well. Add additional mayonnaise if necessary to make sure all macaroni is coated. Add peas and blend, being careful not to smash the peas. Add salt and pepper to taste. (If the bacon is very salty, additional salt may not be necessary.) Flavors blend well if allowed to stand refrigerated several hours or overnight. Additional mayonnaise may have to be added just before serving, as the macaroni absorbs it while standing. Garnish with parsley, or hard-boiled egg slices before serving. Makes 12–16 side servings.

The Collector's Page

BUDDY HOLLY

For information on how to order this Rock 'n' Roll/ Rhythm and Blues Commemorative Stamp, please see page 2.

3

Vegetarian Entrees

Surf Man Vegetarian Stir Fry
Hot And Spicy Cauliflower A Go Go
Lightnin' Strikes Lugee's Linguini
The Mountain's High Crunch
String Beans Patti La Belle
Indonesian Salad With Spicy Peanut Dressing
Jeff Ament's Hack Thai Peanut Curry Thang

The Beach Boys
Bruce Johnston

Brian Wilson turned a suburban California garage band into The Beach Boys, a group that changed and enhanced Rock & Roll forever with their uniquely all-American sound. With such classics as "Little Deuce Coupe," "Surfin'," "Good Vibrations," "California Girls" and "God Only Knows," Brian, Dennis and Carl Wilson (all brothers), Mike Love and Al Jardine were the boys next door who personified the upbeat, laid-back sunny Southern California life-style.

"Surfin'"went almost nowhere on the small label it was originally released on, so the Wilsons' father, Murray, took their recordings to other record companies and, finally interested Capitol Records.

"Surfin' Safari," backed with "409," reached the Top 20, and endless smash hits followed. The Beach Boys' first number-one hit, "I Get Around," sold over a million copies, and the band debuted on The Ed Sullivan Show in October 1964.

Brian Wilson suffered the first of many breakdowns in 1965 and was replaced briefly by Glen Campbell before Bruce Johnston came aboard, making his debut in New Orleans. Despite his problems, Brian continued with the band, and in January 1966, he began work on what would be regarded as his recording zenith:*Pet Sounds*. This record set new standards for the group and was critically acclaimed as its best work yet. That is, until "Good Vibrations" was released in December, which was critically rated as the group's best-ever recording. Despite the untimely drowning death of drummer Dennis, The Beach Boys continued recording and producing hits, and were inducted into the Rock & Roll Hall Of Fame in 1988. That same year, the band hit number one again with "Kokomo," a song featured in the Tom Cruise movie, *Cocktail*. It had been over 24 years since their first hit—the longest span ever achieved in the rock era.

Surf Man Vegetarian Stir Fry

2 Tbsp olive oil
1/2 lb mushrooms, sliced
2 ears corn (or equivalent)
6–8 carrots, sliced
1 package firm Tofu, cut up

1/4 lb zucchini, sliced
1/2 clove garlic, pressed
1/4 onion, chopped
Small amount marinade sauce
   (for extra flavor)

Sauté mushrooms, garlic and onions in olive oil. Steam carrots and corn, then add to sauté mixture. Add remaining ingredients and season to taste with Spike or Vegit. Mix all for under 5 minutes. Serve on a bed of rice. Serves 6.

Belinda Carlisle

Ten years ago, Belinda Carlisle secured her place in the Rock & Roll history books as the lead singer of The Go Go's, the first and only all female band to land a simultaneous number-one single, "Our Lips are Sealed," and album, *Beauty and the Beat*, on the *Billboard* charts. As a solo artist, her 1986 gold-certified debut LP, *Belinda*, featured the Top 5 single, "Mad About You," which launched a newly svelte, sophisticated Carlisle in a video that also starred her husband, Morgan Mason. She has scored a string of hits, including her Grammy-nominated number one "Heaven Is A Place On Earth" and "I Get Weak." Her subsequent albums—*Heaven On Earth, Runaway Horses* and *Live Your Life To Be Free*—have sold over five million copies worldwide.

"I think this is my calling," Belinda explains. "When I was around nine or ten, I would spend the summer sitting on the porch and listening to the Top 40—The Beach Boys, The Mamas and Papas, The Fifth Dimension, The Guess Who and Bobby Sherman from about nine in the morning until about six or seven o'clock." In the late '70s when the punk scene came along, Belinda seized the moment. "That was when I really worked hard at getting a band together. And because everybody that was in a band in that period was pretty terrible, it was easy!"

Belinda gave birth to a baby boy, James Duke Mason, in April 1992 while the riots raged in Los Angeles. "It was a terrifying experience," Belinda recalls. "The day after I had the baby, I was looking out the window in my room and watching at least a dozen fires burning all around Los Angeles. It was strange on one hand to be joyous at the birth of my son, but sad on the other hand by the chaos and devastation going on in the streets not far from the hospital." Belinda is soon to release her fourth solo album.

Hot And Spicy Cauliflower A Go Go

1/2 cup olive oil
1/3 cup gingerroot, chopped and peeled
1 bulb garlic, whole peeled cloves
1 heaping tsp each of tumeric, Garam
   Masala (get at Indian grocery store),
   curry powder, crushed red chilies

1 tsp salt
2 jalapeno chilies, cut into quarters
2–3 tomatoes, peeled and cut into
   quarters
2 medium cauliflower, cut into large
   bite-sized pieces

Heat olive oil in large skillet over medium-high flame. Add gingerroot (it's great for the immune system, by the way) and sauté 3–4 minutes. Add whole peeled garlic cloves and cook 2 more minutes, stirring constantly. Add spices, then add tomatoes and cauliflower pieces. Lower heat to medium and cook, stirring occasionally, until tomatoes are saucy and the cauliflower can easily be pierced with a fork. Sometimes (usually) I feel fat and just sauté with Pam and water—but, of course, it's not as good.

"This curry is not for the timid of tongue!"

Lou Christie

Lou's artistic beginnings read like something out of an "Andy Hardy" movie where Mickey Rooney says to Judy Garland, "Hey! Let's put on a show. We can use Dad's garage!" The legend began at the family pizza parlor, where Lou, along with his sister Amy and two other friends, formed The Crewnecks. At an audition with The Crewnecks, he met Twyla Herbert—a wildly eccentric musical talent who was the pianist at the audition. Pardon the pun, but lightnin' struck! Together, Lou and Twyla began a career right at the audition by writing their first song together in just fifteen minutes. The next day they were in a two-track studio with their collaboration, "The Gypsy Cried." It seemed that overnight Lou Sacco from the pizza parlor became Lou Christie, million-selling recording artist.

Success followed success with hits such as "Two Faces Have I," "Lightnin' Strikes," "Rhapsody In The Rain" and "I'm Gonna Make You Mine." Among the highlights of Lou's career is a tour with the "Dick Clark Caravan of Stars" with Diana Ross. They shared billing on the concert tour that consisted of 72 one-nighters in a row—possibly a record! Another highlight is a Royal Command Performance while living in London.

Today, Lou makes his home in New York City and performs in concerts and clubs throughout the United States and Europe. He has shared with us his special recipe for "Lightnin' Strikes Lugee's Linguini" and suggests, "Always open a bottle of Italian wine before you start to cook! Once that's established, everything gets better and better—just like life in Italy."

Lightnin' Strikes Lugee's Linguini

3 or 4 cloves garlic, diced or sliced
1/4 cup olive oil
4–5 big tomatoes, cut up

5–6 fresh basil leaves
Salt and pepper
1 lb linguini

Brown garlic slowly in olive oil. Add tomatoes, basil and salt and pepper. Cover and sauté over low heat for 10–15 minutes. Boil enough water (salted and oiled) for linguini. Cook linguini *al dente* (firm). Pour marvelous sauce over linguini and serve. Open another bottle of wine. *"Buona Fortuna!"*

Dick and Dee Dee
Dick and Sandy St. John

The act, Dick and Dee Dee, began its recording career on Liberty Records in the summer of 1961. Dick wrote "The Mountain's High" in April, and by August it was number two in the nation. The driving forces behind the duo were actually Dick St. John—who sang the lead, falsetto and some harmony parts—and the genius of producer/arranger Donald Ralke. During the '60s, they had a total of fourteen chart records including "Tell Me," "Young And In Love," "Turn Around" and "Thou Shalt Not Steal."

Sandy and Dick were married in 1966, and Sandy joined Dick as part of the duo in 1969, replacing the first "Dee Dee," who was actually named Mary. During the 1970s, the St. Johns devoted most of their time to songwriting—working as staff writers for publishers such as Chappell Music, Screen Gems, Shapiro Bernstein and The Filmways Corporation (now Orion Pictures). They wrote songs for numerous TV films and rediscovered country music. With Chuck Tharp of The Fireballs, Sandy co-wrote the number-one Johnny Duncan hit, "Sweet Country Woman." Also, during the '70s their songs were recorded by Sha Na Na, R. B. Greaves, Vicki Lawrence, Johnny Paycheck, Cilla Black, Joey Scarsbury and many others. Donny and Marie Osmond did a remake of Dick's song "Young And In Love" (the Dick and Dee Dee hit), and Dick also wrote the smash single "Yellow Balloon."

Today, the St. Johns live in Pacific Palisades, California, and continue to perform on the "oldies circuit" throughout the United States. During a tour a few years ago, Sandy got the idea for this cookbook while taking note of what Rock & Rollers would eat while on the road. Sandy and Dick have been involved with The National Music Foundation since 1988 and have been working on the cookbook for over two years. They have been into eating cruelty-free food for nearly 25 years and have been students of metaphysics for just as long. On June 16, 1993, they had the distinct honor of unveiling the Bill Haley Rock 'n' Roll/Rhythm and Blues Commemorative Stamp in an official U.S. Postal Service ceremony presided over by Dick Clark.

The Mountain's High Crunch (A Hill Of A Cruelty-Free Entrée)

The "Crunch" should be made individually. The ingredients necessary to make one entree are:

4 rice cakes
2 Tbsp raw almonds, sliced

2 tsp mayonnaise
Garlic powder, to taste
1 medium tomato, diced
1 cup monterey jack cheese, grated
Sesame seeds

Step one:
Break up two of the rice cakes into small pieces. Add 1 Tbsp sliced raw almonds and mix. Blend in 1 tsp mayonnaise and sprinkle with garlic powder. Mix thoroughly and press into bottom of an individual baking/serving dish (approximately 6" in diameter).

Step two:
Sprinkle diced tomato over top of mixture. Sprinkle 1/2 cup grated jack cheese over the top. Repeat step one and press down on top of the cheese-covered tomato. Add the remaining jack cheese evenly over the top and sprinkle with sesame seeds. Bake at 325° until cheese is melted and bubbly. Serve hot.
The "Crunch" can be prepared ahead of time and kept in refrigerator until ready to cook and serve. Once it is "oven-ready," it takes only a few minutes to cook.

Patti La Belle

Born May 24, 1944, in Philadelphia, Patti was raised in the melting pot of Southwest Philly. She lived a happy, wholesome teenage life—running track, singing in the glee club and acting in plays at John Bartram High School. But her extraordinary musical gift emerged most clearly in the Beulah Baptist Church Choir, where she remained a soloist even after embarking on a professional career.

Perhaps more than any other artist in the history of popular music, the distinctive Patti La Belle has been true to herself in every varied phase of her musical career. In the '60s, she led the superstar "girl group" Patti La Belle and The Bluebells; in the '70s, she was the driving force of rock's first all-female band, La Belle; and in the '80s, her talent as a solo artist dominated the music scene. Patti has had numerous hits—from "I Sold My Heart To The Junkman," "Down The Aisle" and "Danny Boy" with the Bluebells, to "Lady Marmalade" and "The Revolution Will Not Be Televised" with La Belle, to her solo triumphs "New Attitude," "Stir It Up" and "On My Own."

On a more personal but equally important note, Patti served as the spokeswoman for The National Cancer Institute to help alert women to the importance of early breast cancer detection. Working to defeat breast cancer, which claimed the lives of Patti's mother and three sisters, is a cause to which she is passionately dedicated. Patti is the first to remind everyone that her most important role is that of wife and mother (she's "Mom" to one teenage boy, two adopted sons in their twenties and the son and daughter of her late sister Jackie). When she's not setting the world on its ear, she's home (still Philadelphia) cooking, shopping, doing laundry and, she says, "being a person—just like everyone else!"

String Beans Patti La Belle
(String Beans With A New Attitude)

1–5 lbs fresh string beans
2 large cans whole tomatoes
1 large can tomato paste
8 cloves garlic, chopped
3 large onions
4 Tbsp olive oil

1 lb provolone cheese, shredded
1 lb mozzarella cheese, shredded
Oregano
Lawry's seasoned salt
Fresh pepper

Steam beans till bright green and still a little crunchy. In a large pan, warm tomatoes and tomato paste. Gently sauté garlic and onions in olive oil until they are translucent. Add garlic and onions to tomatoes. Season with oregano, Lawry's and fresh pepper to taste. In a large pan, pour down a layer of sauce, add green beans, shredded provolone, more sauce, beans and mozzarella, and so on. Make 3–4 layers. Continue to cook on top of stove until all cheese has melted.

k.d. lang

Born and raised in Consort, Alberta, Kathy Dawn Lang began playing guitar at age ten, and within three years was writing and performing her own original works.

In the early '80s, k.d. formed her own band, the reclines, and drew enthusiastic response for their expressive and emotionally charged performances, not to mention her exquisite voice. The band's first single, "Friday Dance Promenade," was followed by the independently released album, *A Truly Western Experience*. By 1984, the group had signed to Sire Records which released *Angel With A Lariat* in 1987 to wide acclaim.

k.d.'s next album, *Shadowland* earned her a gold album, *Rolling Stone's* Critic's Pick for Best Female Singer, Canada's Juno and CASY awards for Best Female Vocalist and a Grammy for Best Vocal Collaboration for "Crying," her duet with Roy Orbison. In 1989, *Absolute Torch And Twang*, k.d.'s fourth album, earned her the Grammy for Best Female Vocalist.

After bending and stretching the boundaries of country music, k.d. moved boldly into unexplored musical territory with her fifth album, *Ingenue*—a direct, sultry, melancholy and sometimes heartbreaking musical experience.

How does k.d. want her music to affect her fans? "I would hope that it would be a gut level reaction and that my lyrics are general enough that fans can apply them to their own situations. I hope that the music moves the listeners in their own way as much as it moved me to write it."

Indonesian Salad With Spicy Peanut Dressing (k.d.'s Constant Craving)

For the salad:
3 Tbsp vegetable oil
Salt to taste
1 lb firm tofu, patted dry and cut
  into 1/4" cubes
2 small potatoes, boiled and
  cut into bite-sized wedges
1/2 lb fresh spinach, cleaned,
  steamed, and chopped
1/2 small head green cabbage,
  shredded and lightly steamed

1/2 lb mung bean sprouts,
  washed thoroughly

For the dressing:
4 cloves garlic
1/4 cup roasted peanuts
5 tsp soy sauce or tamari
3 Tbsp lime or lemon juice
4 tsp brown sugar
1/4 tsp cayenne pepper
2 Tbsp water

Heat the oil and salt in a medium frying pan over medium heat. Add the tofu in small batches and sauté until lightly browned on both sides, about 5 minutes. Remove with a slotted spoon and drain on paper towel.

Arrange the tofu, potatoes, spinach and cabbage together on individual serving plates. Prepare dressing by placing all dressing ingredients in a blender and blending until smooth. If dressing seems too thick, add another teaspoon of water. Top the vegetables and tofu with the bean sprouts and dressing, and serve immediately. Serves 6.

Pearl Jam
Jeff Ament

Born and bred in Seattle, Washington, Pearl Jam began in the mid '80s as Green River with Stone Gossard on guitar and Jeff Ament on bass. This band and its three Sub Pop albums formed a fountainhead of inspiration for the post-punk Northwest rock scene.

After the breakup of Green River, Stone and Jeff moved on to another influential Seattle band, Mother Love Bone. The release of their major-label debut, *Apple*, coincided with the untimely death of lead singer Andrew Wood. Even though *Apple* appeared on many critics' "Ten Best" lists for 1990, Mother Love Bone broke up and Stone and Jeff left to form Pearl Jam with Mike McCready, Dave Abbruzzese and Eddie Vedder.

Ten, the epic debut album by Pearl Jam quickly became an exciting, very successful addition to the burgeoning "Seattle Sound"—selling millions of albums and creating zillions of fans.

Jeff Ament's Hack Thai Peanut Curry Thang

2–3 heaping tsp curry (your choice)
4 oz coconut milk
2 oz soy sauce
1 small pkg peanuts, crushed
3 huge Tbsp crunchy peanut butter

Spoonful of ginger, grated
Lots of garlic
1–3 tsp red chilies (or as many as you can handle)

After you have mixed the above ingredients in a bowl, chop up your favorite colorful vegetables and carcass (if you must). (Tiger prawns make a weird little scream when you throw 'em in hot oil.) Stir-fry in huge pan or wok with 2 Tbsp sesame oil for 1 minute on high heat.

Dump into pot with special sauce, simmer for 1 minute and serve over rice.

Buy a six-pack of Singha beer and eat with chopsticks for authenticity. While cooking, listen to Tom Waits. While eating, Eno is cool.

The Collector's Page

CLYDE McPHATTER

For information on how to order this Rock 'n' Roll/ Rhythm and Blues Commemorative Stamp, please see page 2.

4
Seafood Entrees

The Great Kahuna's Crab Sauce With Pasta

Zip A Dee Doo Dah Catfish

Slippery Shrimp Scampi Parmesan

Hey! Baby, Try A Fish Fillet

XS-ively Delicious Pla Rad Prik

Michael Hutchence's Original Sin

Shrimp Purlo

Creole Fish Fillets From The Sea of Love

Come And Get Your Shrimp

Fillet Of Soul Fish Cakes

Joe Walsh's Good Old-Fashioned Tuna Fish Casserole

**Stay For Dinner, Little Darlin',
And I'll Make Catfish Stew**

Frankie Avalon

One of America's most popular entertainers, Frankie Avalon went from a '50s teen idol to a national and international star. Born in Philadelphia, Frankie's early career as a trumpet player ended abruptly when a family friend, Bob Marcucci, heard him sing and signed him to a record contract. His first song, "De De Dinah," became a smash hit, and his recording of "Venus" was one of the biggest selling hits of the era. As Frankie's popularity as a recording artist grew, he appeared on *American Bandstand*, *The Ed Sullivan Show* and numerous other TV programs, and toured the country with the hottest acts of the day.

Frankie's career took another turn as a movie actor. He appeared in over two dozen movies, starring with Alan Ladd in *Guns Of The Timberland* and playing opposite John Wayne in *The Alamo*. Some of his many other film credits include *Voyage To The Bottom Of The Sea*, *Grease* and the popular '60s beach movies—*Beach Party*, *Muscle Beach Party*, *Beach Blanket Bingo* and *Bikini Beach*—in which he became half of one of the most famous cinematic couples in history: Frankie and Annette. In 1987, he reunited with Annette Funicello and made the hit movie *Back to the Beach*.

Frankie remains a highly popular attraction in Las Vegas, Atlantic City, Reno and Tahoe and takes his act to clubs, parks, fairs and other venues across America and around the world.

Apart from his busy work schedule, Frankie is an avid golfer and lives in Los Angeles with his wife Kay, to whom he has been married since 1963. They have eight children.

The Great Kahuna's Crab Sauce With Pasta

1 cup olive oil
1 whole Dungeness crab,
　cleaned and lightly cracked
1 large can crushed tomatoes

1 large can tomato sauce
Garlic powder
Pepper
1 lb pasta

In a large pot, sauté crab and garlic powder in olive oil for 5 minutes. Then add tomatoes, tomato sauce, more garlic powder and pepper. Put lid on pot halfway and cook for 45 minutes.

Boil pasta. (One pound of spaghetti feeds 4 people.) Pour sauce over cooked spaghetti and take out crab. The crab becomes the side dish to eat along with your pasta.

Bob B. Soxx & The Blue Jeans
Bobby Sheen

Bobby Sheen ("Bob B. Soxx") was, and still is, one of those great natural singers. He grew up on the West Coast and began singing at a very early age. His unique, identifiable voice has supplied background vocals on many great records, giving them that extra-special sound.

In 1962, Bobby teamed up with Fanita James and Darlene Love to form the group Bob B. Soxx & The Blue Jeans. At that time, record producer Phil Spector was just coming into his great "wall of sound." He took Fanita, Darlene and Bobby into the studio to record "Zip A Dee Doo Dah"— the song featured in the old Walt Disney film, *Song Of The South*. It was an instant hit featuring the voices of these three great singers. When Bobby's voice cut in, you knew what a great voice could do for any producer.

Bobby was also featured on Phil Spector's classic Christmas album singing, oddly enough, a song that has nothing to do with Christmas: "The White Cliffs Of Dover." But, once again, he gave a phenomenal performance.

In 1990, we did a tour to Alaska with Bobby on the show. He's just as good today as he was in days gone by. And when you try his recipe for "Zip A Dee Doo Dah Catfish" you'll find that Bobby is also an excellent cook!

Zip A Dee Doo Dah Catfish

3 Tbsp Dijon mustard
2 Tbsp milk

4 farm-raised catfish fillets
1 cup ground pecans

Combine mustard and milk in small bowl. Dip fillets in mustard mixture, then dip in ground pecans, coating thoroughly. Shake off excess nuts. Place fish on greased baking sheet. Bake at 500° for 10–12 minutes or until fish flakes. Makes 4 servings.

Bon Jovi
David Bryan

"Even if Elton John was my piano player, Jeff Beck my guitarist and Kenny Aronoff my drummer, it wouldn't be the same turning around and not seeing the guys that believed in me when I told them we were going to make it back in 1982," says Jon Bon Jovi. He adds, "When the five of us are together, it's magic because it's fun."

Back then, the boys from New Jersey had no idea what the future held for them. They began as a live band, gaining a solid reputation on the hard rock circuit while developing material for their self-titled debut album. Their second album, *7800° Fahrenheit*, released in 1985, went gold. In 1986, they broke through with *Slippery When Wet*. Its first single, "You Give Love A Bad Name," was the group's first number-one hit, selling more than a million copies and taking the album to the top of the charts for eight weeks in 1986. "Livin' On A Prayer" and "Wanted Dead Or Alive" put *Slippery* back at number one for seven weeks in 1987. The group headlined the annual Monsters of Rock Festival at Castle Donington, Leicester, England, and closed the year as the world's most popular rock group. Resting after their 130-date "Tour Without End," the group went back into the studio to record 1988's *New Jersey*, which spawned the hit singles "Bad Medicine," "Born To Be My Baby," "I'll Be There For You," "Lay Your Hands On Me" and "Living In Sin." After ending their 237-show, sixteen-month world tour, the group took a hiatus, with members Jon Bon Jovi and Richie Sambora recording solo efforts.

Their most recent effort, *Keep The Faith*, captures the band at an important crossroads, a fact of which Jon Bon Jovi is well aware. "We can save the world. But first we've got to start with ourselves. If you believe in yourself, anything in the world is possible."

Slippery Shrimp Scampi Parmesan

1 lb tiger shrimps, cleaned
Extra virgin olive oil
Butter
Garlic

1 jar Prego spaghetti sauce
Fresh Italian herbs
Grated mozzarella cheese

Lightly sauté herbs, garlic and shrimp in oil and a drop of butter. Remove from heat. Pour sauce into Pyrex baking dish. Place shrimp on top of sauce, cover with a thick coat of mozzarella cheese and bake until cheese melts. This is especially good served over angel hair pasta.

Bruce Channel

Bruce first began singing and entertaining in Texas when he was still in his early teens, performing mostly at local dances. In 1962, he discovered a small recording studio in town and decided to make a demo of some songs he had written. At the last minute, he substituted a brand-new song he had just finished called "Hey! Baby." Six months later, Bruce watched in awe as this record soared to number one on the charts and stayed there for three weeks.

Thus began a long and fascinating career in the United States and England. At the height of his popularity, Bruce headlined a show in England featuring a then relatively unknown group—The Beatles! After more than a decade of touring and recording, Bruce grew tired of the road and returned to Fort Worth to settle down with his wife, Christine, whom he had met in England. He decided to leave the music scene for a while.

In 1978, Bruce moved to Nashville and began writing songs for country recording artists. Since then, his success as a writer includes number-one records for T. G. Shep-

herd, Janie Fricke, John Conlee and Mel McDaniel. Anne Murray's remake of "Hey! Baby" was a smash. He has also had cuts recorded by Alabama, The Oak Ridge Boys, Jerry Lee Lewis and Tom Jones.

Bruce received an award from BMI for one million radio performances of "Hey! Baby," and the classic is featured in the movie, *Dirty Dancing*. Today, he still lives in Nashville and remains actively involved in songwriting and music publishing.

Hey! Baby, Try A Fish Fillet

1 Fish
1 Potato
Oil

Fillet fish, not more than 1/2" thick. Wash fillet in fresh water. Place wet fillet on plate. (Season if you want.) Slice potato paper thin. Lay fillet on large, broad cake knife or spatula and cover with potato slices. Turn fillet over onto another cake knife or spatula and cover the other side with potato slices. Heat oil in pan ready for frying. Cook until potatoes are brown and done. Incredible as it may seem, the fish will be cooked perfectly. Serve with lemon wedges and favorite vegetables or salad. Serves 1.

INXS
John Farriss and Michael Hutchence

The story of INXS begins in the Australian pubs—sweaty, airless places crammed so tight with people that "we'd have to suck away at oxygen cannisters in between songs just so we could keep playing," recalls singer Michael Hutchence. The musical journey that followed resulted in a string of multi-million selling albums and sold-out gigs all over the world.

Originally formed in 1977 as The Farriss Brothers, the lineup of INXS remains unchanged to this day. Straight out of high school, they started writing, rehearsing and playing local hotels and pubs, virtually seven nights a week! In 1979 they changed their name to INXS and in 1980 released their self-titled first album.

After four huge albums in Australia and Europe, INXS landed their first U.S. Top 5 pop single, "What You Need,"

from their first U.S. million seller, *Listen Like Thieves*. In 1987 came *Kick*, which sold over four million copies in the United States and another five million worldwide and produced four Top 10 singles on the *Billboard* pop charts. *X* followed, then *Live Baby Live* and their newest effort, *Welcome To Wherever You Are*.

In March 1992, INXS made history when they organized the biggest rock concert in Australian history, raising more than half a million dollars for AIDS research.

When asked to ponder the proverbial rock question, "How do you want to be remembered in the history books?" Michael Hutchence responds: "As a very good pop band, at least! Because the bottom line is that we don't get too precious about things—we're Australian after all!"

XS-ively Delicious Pla Rad Prik

1 lb whole fish, cleaned
1 Tbsp white rice wine
1/2 cup all-purpose plain flour
4 cups oil for deep-frying

Sauce:
5 Tbsp oil
6 or 7 cloves garlic, crushed and minced
1/4 cup green bell pepper/capsicum,
    chopped into tiny pieces

1/4 cup red bell pepper/capsicum,
    chopped into tiny pieces
1/2 cup onions, finely chopped
1/4 cup fish sauce
1/8 cup oyster sauce
1 red hot chili pepper (no, not the
    band!) If you want it mildly hot, only
    use 1/2 pepper and make sure to take
    out the seeds.
4 Tbsp sugar
2–3 Tbsp Ketchup

Cut 3 diagonal slashes to the bone on each side of the fish, then sprinkle it with rice wine. Flour fish on all sides. Heat oil to 350° and carefully immerse the fish into the hot oil. Deep-fry fish until golden brown (about 6 or so minutes on each side). While fish is cooking, heat a medium wok or skillet. Add oil, then garlic.

Before garlic turns light brown, add onion. Then add green and red pepper, chili pepper, sugar, fish sauce, oyster sauce and ketchup. Mix. Taste sauce to see if it's okay. If it's too hot, add more sugar. Place fish on serving dish and pour the sauce on top.

Michael Hutchence's Original Sin

I bumped into Michael at a party and asked him for a recipe. He said that he didn't cook but his favorite thing to eat was the following medley. As often as he can, he flies to Paris for the weekend and on Saturday night sits down at a café to indulge in this seafood feast:

Raw oysters
Langoustino
Fresh mayonnaise
Lemon
Gallons of red wine

Lynyrd Skynyrd
Dale Rossington and Michael Lewis

The release in June 1991 of *Lynyrd Skynyrd 1991* marked the return to the recording studio of one of the most critically acclaimed, commercially successful Rock & Roll bands to emerge from the heart of the American South. Hailing from Jacksonville, Florida, the original Skynyrd forged a trademark sound that melded the influences of late '60s British rock with traditional blues and country roots. As Rolling Stone commented, "In matters of unpretentiousness, power and invention, the best hard rock band in America during the first half of the 1970s may well have been Lynyrd Skynyrd." Along with several Top Ten albums, Skynyrd had smash singles with "Free Bird," a tribute to Duane Allman, "Sweet Home Alabama" and the haunting "That Smell."

In October 1977, a tragic plane crash cut Skynyrd's career short in its prime—killed were vocalist/co-founder Ronnie Van Zant and guitarist Steve Gaines. The survivors decided to lay the Skynyrd soul to rest.

As the tenth anniversary of the plane crash approached, several Skynyrd members began discussing the possibility of a reunion concert. After some serious soul searching, Johnny Van Zant, brother of Ronnie, was enlisted to take over the lead vocal spot on the Tribute Tour. The first reunion gig turned into a full-fledged tour, and the Lynyrd Skynyrd spirit was rekindled. What had really taken place was the full-fledged reformation of Lynyrd Skynyrd.

This year marks the twentieth anniversary of the release of the first Lynyrd Skynyrd album, and they have just released *The Last Rebel*.

Shrimp Purlo

1/2 lb bacon
1 white onion, chopped
2 bell peppers, chopped
1 clove garlic, crushed
1 large can skinless tomatoes

3 lbs raw medium-sized shrimp
1 large bag rice
  (regular long cooking rice)
Water, twice the amount of rice

Cook the bacon in a large skillet. Just use the bacon grease—toss out the bacon. Sauté the chopped onion, bell pepper and garlic in the bacon grease until onion loses its color and bell pepper softens. Add skinless tomatoes. Pan-fry on low until almost all of the moisture is gone (approximately 45 minutes). Add rice and water. Bring to a hard boil, stirring constantly. Reduce to low heat. Add the shrimp. Cover for 1 1/2–2 minutes. Stir once more to avoid sticking. Cover again and simmer for 25 minutes. Optional: garnish with Datilo-do-it hot sauce.

Phil Phillips

"Sea of Love" had to be the sexiest romantic hit in the summer of 1959.

Phil Phillips, born Philip Baptiste in Lake Charles, Louisiana, grew up singing gospel music and was raised in a strict, religious household. While in high school, he formed a group called The Gateway Quartet. They spent their free time after school and on weekends singing in community churches, and became very popular with everyone who heard them. This led to a few local TV performances that added to their popularity.

Then, in the late '50s, R & B acts became the fad around the Lake Charles area (and probably everywhere else, too). Phil knew one of the greatest zydeco musicians, the late Clifton Chenier, whose uncle sat down with Phil and taught him how to tune the guitar. With this knowledge and using basic chords in a Spanish style, Phil wrote "Sea of Love." A short time later he was introduced to the owner of a small record company right in his hometown of Lake Charles. The rest is history: the record was an instant smash hit, and Phil was greeted by cheering crowds who loved his song when he joined a national tour with the Dick Clark Caravan of Stars.

Like many other artists from the '50s and '60s, Phil feels that he was never appropriately compensated for his hit. That's one reason for his interest in The National Music Foundation. Today, a very religious man, he still makes his home in Louisiana with Winnie, his wife of many years.

Creole Fish Fillets From The Sea Of Love

2 1/4 lbs fish fillets

Batter:
1 cup evaporated milk
2 eggs, slightly beaten
2 tsp seasoned salt
1/2 tsp dry cayenne pepper
1 tsp basil leaves

1/2 tsp garlic, minced
1 tsp onion, minced

Flour Mixture:
1 cup plain flour
1 1/2 cups yellow corn meal
1 tsp seasoned salt
1/2 tsp cayenne pepper

Rinse fish fillets and pat dry. Arrange in shallow dish. Combine batter ingredients and mix well. Pour over fish fillets, coating evenly. Refrigerate 1 hour, turning occasionally. Combine flour mixture in plastic or paper bag. Add fillets and shake to cover with mixture. Pour about 2 quarts of oil in a deep heavy pot and heat to about 375°. Fry until golden brown, about 5–8 minutes or until done. Transfer fried fillets to paper towel to drain excess oil. Serve with cream potatoes and your favorite vegetables, hot cayenne sauce and ketchup.

Redbone
Patrick and Lolly Vegas

Redbone takes their name from an old Cajun word meaning "Native American"—a name aptly selected by Patrick and Lolly Vegas, as these two brothers heading the group are Yaqui Indians of the Mexican Nation. Pat and Lolly grew up listening to their grandfather play the guitar, and a few years later Pat was playing bass and Lolly lead guitar. When Pat was only fifteen he and older brother Lolly moved to the Monterey Peninsula where they teamed up with three other musicians. After a while they felt that they were in a "rut" and could only grow by moving on. Guided by the spirit of their ancestors, they migrated to Los Angeles. Confident and talented, Pat and Lolly sought work in all the local clubs, but since they were minors, they had no luck. Down to their last three dollars, they saw a poster advertising a concert by a group called The Down Beats. They had known a band by this name up in Monterey, and if this was the same group, they knew it was possible this might lead to a job! Well, it was the same band and within hours the Vegas brothers had not only been invited to join the group, but also to share living quarters in a huge mansion. Everything was working!

Fascinated by music, Pat and Lolly hung around the American Recording Studio in Hollywood. Eventually their perseverance won out and they were allowed to participate in some studio ses-

sions. For the next three years they played sessions for such noted artists as Frank Sinatra, Elvis Presley and Sonny and Cher. This finally led to the formation of Redbone and the release of their own CBS/Epic LP, *Witch Queen of New Orleans*. Their single, "Come And Get Your Love," sold seven million copies and remained number one for fourteen weeks.

Come And Get Your Shrimp

2 lbs large tiger shrimp, tail on
2 cups half and half
1/2 cup dry white wine
1/4 cup cognac
1 large garlic clove minced
1 Tbsp brown sugar
1 pinch nutmeg

1 tsp Hungarian paprika
1 large white onion, minced
1 tsp fresh cilantro, minced
1 pinch cumin
1 stick salted butter
About 20 red flame grapes, peeled

Heat butter in large skillet over medium heat. Add garlic, onion, brown sugar and shrimp. When shrimp is lightly browned (about 2 minutes), add wine and cognac, then add the half and half. Now add the paprika, red flame grapes and cilantro and reduce heat to low. Let simmer for 20 minutes and add the cumin and nutmeg. Simmer for another 10 minutes. Can be served over white rice or egg noodles, with oven-heated and buttered French or Italian bread and wine of choice. *Bon appétit!*

Soul Asylum
Grant Young

After two years in the basement and the garage, Soul Asylum hooked up with Twin/Tone records in 1983 while still performing under the name Loud Fast Rules. When the album *Say What You Will* was completed, they came out of the studio as Soul Asylum and started almost ten years of non-stop touring, grabbing Soul Asylum fans in every major U.S. city. After several albums on three different labels, they landed on Sony Records to record their most recent and biggest hit record, *Grave Dancer's Union*, which generated the raucous smash single "Somebody To Shove." "It was recorded ten minutes after the band learned it," lead guitarist Dan Murphy remembers. "It's completely spontaneous!"

For over a decade, the four Minneapolis natives have somehow endured the ups and downs of life on the road and still manage to enjoy each other's company. "For about three or four years we toured by van, sleeping on peoples' floors," Dan recalls. "As a unit, it's pretty amazing how we get along." The chemistry that exists between band members is "something that can't be taken for granted," says frontman Dave Pirner. "We think it's really important to the fiber of the group—we've grown up together and become an entity. We're still great friends and love playing. It's as amazing to us as to anyone else." *The Village Voice* has christened Soul Asylum the "Best Live Band in America." "It's a bonding thing with the people who come and see you," bassist Karl Mueller says. "I love meeting new people and seeing new things on the road."

Fillet Of Soul Fish Cakes

1/2 lb shrimp, peeled and de-veined
1/2 lb fish
3 scallions, thinly sliced
3–4 Kaffir lime leaves, minced
Lime juice (for taste)
1 heaping Tbsp red curry paste
Breadcrumbs
Oil (for frying)

Dipping Sauce:
1 cup granulated sugar
1 cup rice vinegar
1 1/2 tsp salt
1/2 cucumber, quartered and thinly
  sliced
1/2 bunch cilantro, minced
Chili paste (to taste)
Fresh-roasted ground peanuts (to taste)

Grind shrimp and fish together. Add scallions, lime leaves, lime juice and curry paste. Combine. Add enough bread crumbs to soak up excess juice and hold the fish-cakes together, but not too much as to dry them out. Shape them into patties, toss them lightly in more bread crumbs and fry until done. Drain on paper towels. Serve with the dipping sauce recipe included below, or whatever strikes you at the moment.

Dipping Sauce:
Combine the sugar, vinegar and salt in a small saucepan; heat until the sugar dissolves. Remove from heat and cool to room temperature. Add remaining ingredients. Serve.

Joe Walsh

Will the real Joe Walsh please stand up? Through four albums with his legendary first band, The James Gang, three albums as a member of The Eagles and ten solo efforts (including his latest, *Songs For A Dying Planet*), the veteran rocker from Wichita, Kansas, has tried on a number of different faces.

Joe Walsh grew up in the Midwest and attended Kent State University in Ohio during the student demonstrations that

left four people shot to death by the National Guard. It was there that Joe founded The James Gang, the seminal power trio which drew praise from the likes of Pete Townshend (who chose them to open The Who's 1971 European tour).

As well known for his diverse guitar work—augmented by the late Duane Allman's special slide technique—as his singing/songwriting, Joe joined The Eagles in 1976 for the blockbuster *Hotel California*, co-writing the classic "Life In The Fast Lane." That experience later led to his savage lampoon of rock star excess, "Life's Been Good." After two more Eagles albums, the band broke up, but Walsh continued with a succession of solo albums including the satirical *There Goes The Neighborhood*, featuring the infamous shot of Joe astride a tank.

Along the way, Walsh ran for President in 1980 with the slogan "Free gas for everyone!" which succeeded in registering one million new voters long before "Rock the Vote."

Today, fans still sing Joe's famous Hotel California guitar solo (played with Glenn Frey) note for note(!), and he was a showstopper on Ringo Starr's All-Star Band tour. His passion still shines on *Songs For A Dying Planet*—he makes a bid for the Vice Presidency in the satirical "Vote For Me"—and Joe shows no signs of slowing down.

Joe Walsh's Good Old-Fashioned Tuna Fish Casserole

O.K. This is foolproof. Trust me. Here's what you do—

2 cat food-sized cans of tuna fish (the kind packed in water, not oil)

1 bag seashell-shaped noodles
1 can peas
2 cans "golden" mushroom soup
8-pack American Cheese slices

Pre-heat oven to 350°. Get a big pot. Put lots of water, a big spoonful of salt, and just a little bit of cooking oil in it (so just a couple of bubbles of it float around on top of the water). Make it boil. Keep it that way—no lid. When it's boiling, dump in the noodles and stir them around every chance you get. I don't know how long—for example, altitude is a factor (high-altitude pasta takes longer to prepare than sea-level pasta). Just make sure to keep it boiling!! While you're doing that, get a big bowl. Put the "golden" mushroom soup, the peas and the tuna fish (minus the water in the cans they come in) in the bowl. Mix it up so it's all gooshy and the peas are evenly distributed. Every now and then, eat one of the noodles. When they chew like gum, drain all the water out, put some butter in there, and stir it all around until it melts all over the noodles. Dump the pasta into one of those Pyrex cooking things, dump the tuna goosh on top, spread it evenly, and put that in your oven for 25 minutes or so. Stir the whole mess up after 15 minutes. No lid. When it's bubbling like a toxic waste site, layer the cheese on top (4–5 slices), and put whatever it is back in the oven until the cheese is more than melted but less than burnt. It will be very hot! Now carefully, take it out of the oven.

Go tell everybody it's time to eat. I recommend a couple of big old ice cream scoops of it into a big bowl or on a plate, a tossed salad and bread and butter.

Like spaghetti, for some reason it tastes extra special the next day when you heat it back up, either for breakfast or at half-time. Enjoy.

Maurice Williams

Maurice Williams actually started his career several years before his classic hit record, "Stay (Just A Little Bit Longer)," was released. According to *Rolling Stone*, "Stay" was the shortest number-one single in pop music history—1 minute and 37 seconds of pure dynamite!

In 1955, Maurice was a student at Barr Street High School in Lancaster, South Carolina. Along with four other young men, he formed a band called The Royal Charms, changing the name in 1957 to The Gladiolas. Their first record was a song Maurice wrote for the group called "Little Darlin'." It was great, and received immediate airplay for The Gladiolas and became an R & B hit primarily in the South. Then, just a few weeks later, the record was "covered" by The Diamonds, already a very successful group on a major label. Their recording of "Little Darlin'" went on to be a million seller. The song established Maurice as one of the hottest songwriters in the business.

In 1960, the group changed their name again, now becoming Maurice Williams and The Zodiacs. They recorded Maurice's latest composition of "Stay" and it was number one for the entire summer of 1960.

Maurice continued his songwriting career throughout the years. His music has been recorded by a long list of musical greats including Jackson Browne, The Four Seasons and even Elvis Presley.

Maurice Williams and The Zodiacs are still in constant demand and have a full and busy schedule performing in shows all over the world. We're so pleased that he could take a moment to share with us his favorite recipe.

Stay For Dinner, Little Darlin', And I'll Make Catfish Stew

3 lbs catfish fillets
1 flounder fillet
2 onions, cut up
2 cans stewed tomatoes
1 tsp salt

4 cups water
2 cans mixed vegetables
1/2 small cabbage
1/2 lb crabmeat
1/2 lb scallops

Cut up catfish, flounder and onions and put into a large pot. Add tomatoes, water and salt. Bring to a boil and simmer for 45 minutes. Add cabbage, mixed vegetables, crab meat and scallops and continue to simmer for another 30 minutes. Spice it up with hot sauce (optional). Enjoy!

The Collector's Page

ELVIS PRESLEY

For information on how to order this Rock 'n' Roll/ Rhythm and Blues Commemorative Stamp, please see page 2.

5
Poultry Entrees

Boom Boom Cannon's Chicken Cacciatore

Cathy's Favorite Chicken

Sh-Boom Chicken

Da Doo Ron Ron Chicken

Itchy Twitchy Trinidadian Curried Chicken

It's My Party Chicken

Any Day Now I'll Make Roast Chicken In A Dutch Oven

Dancin' In The Street Turkey Sausage Delight

Hey, Hey Pollo

Wild One Chicken

Sleepwalk To The Kitchen And Try Some Garlic Chicken

**Breakin' Up Is Hard to Do—But
Making Mary's Voo Doo Chicken Is Easy**

Doolie's Divine Chicken Thighs

Shepherd's Pie A La Chalky

Miss Holly's Rebel Chicken

Freddy Cannon

Born in Revere, Massachusetts, Freddy Cannon began his career in 1959 when, amazingly enough, he recorded a song written by his own mother! "Tallahassee Lassie" was the beginning of it all—and the first of 22 songs by Freddy to make the *Billboard* charts. This also led to his early appearances on Dick Clark's *American Bandstand*. Few fans realize that Freddy holds the record for the most *American Bandstand* appearances by any performer. He appeared on the show 110 times!

A big thrill for Freddy, and a recent career highlight, was having one of his songs featured in each Bruce Springsteen concert during Bruce's "Tunnel of Love" tour. Every performance by The Boss would open with Freddy's smash, "Palisades Park," pulsating from the speakers on stage. One piece of trivia about "Palisades Park" of which most people aren't aware is that the 1962 hit was written by Chuck Barris, the former host of television's *The Gong Show*.

Freddy makes his home today in Tarzana, California, with his wife of many years, Jeanette. He continues to perform regularly—approximately 125 to 150 concerts annually—including stops at Disneyland, Madison Square Garden and The Greek Theatre in Los Angeles. He's still a dynamic performer and lives up to his nickname of "Boom Boom Cannon," so named because of his driving beat and the "whoos" he yells out (and of course because his name is Cannon!). In his spare time Freddy is an avid Boston Celtics fan, and he doesn't miss a game.

Boom Boom Cannon's Chicken Cacciatore

1/2 cup olive oil
2 cloves garlic, thinly sliced
1 frying chicken (2–3 lbs)
3 1/2 cups (28-oz can) tomatoes
1 1/4 tsp salt

1 tsp oregano
1/2 tsp pepper
1 tsp sugar
1 tsp parsley, chopped
Mushrooms and peppers

Sauté garlic in oil in a large skillet until lightly browned. Rinse chicken and pat dry with paper towels. Place chicken skin down in skillet and brown. Combine tomatoes, salt, oregano, pepper, sugar and parsley. Slowly add mixture to browned chicken. Cook slowly 25–30 minutes or until thickest pieces of chicken are tender when pierced with a fork. If mixture becomes too thick, add a small amount of water. Clean and dice mushrooms and peppers. Sauté in 3 Tbsp butter until lightly browned, then add to chicken and tomato mixture. Mmmm good!

Mike Clifford

Mike Clifford started singing at the young age of five with a group of strolling sidewalk musicians on the island of Catalina, just off the California coast. His late father, Cal Clifford, was a renowned trumpet player with such famous '40s Big Bands as those of Tommy Dorsey, Paul Whiteman and Stan Kenton. Cal later formed his own band, The Cavaliers, and as a teenager Mike sang with them until age fifteen when he signed his first recording contract.

After meeting Mike and hearing his tapes, Helen Noga, the noted personal manager of Johnny Mathis, signed him as a client. She persuaded Ed Sullivan to let Mike perform on *The Ed Sullivan Show*. This "big break" had its down side: Mike missed out on his high school graduation and senior prom. However, the spot on Sullivan's show led to several more appearances and brought Mike to national attention.

A short time later, Mike recorded a song that had been written by Lawrence Welk and George Cates. It was called "Bombay" and became number one in Venezuela. This led to Mike's own TV special on Venevision, the state-owned TV network in Caracas. He then returned to New York in 1962 to sign with United Artists and record his classic romantic ballad "Close To Cathy."

Mike appeared in the first national touring company of the classic Broadway '50s musical, *Grease*, portraying the dual

roles of Johnny Casino and Teen Angel. He also toured with John Travolta in this hit production for almost two years. Then he traveled to Europe to co-star with the legendary French star, Line Renaud, at the Casino de Paris in Paris, France. The show, entitled "Parisline," ran for three years. Mike also sang a duet with Mae West in her last film, *Sextette*, and in the immortal words of the one and only Mae, "his voice really rubs me the right way."

Today, Mike makes his home in Los Angeles, stays creative and busy and remains a very nice and unaffected guy.

Cathy's Favorite Chicken (This Is Why I'm So Close To Her)

3 large boneless chicken breasts
2 eggs, slightly beaten
2 cups seasoned bread crumbs
3 Tbsp olive oil (may need 1 or 2 more,
   depending on chicken size)
1 tsp fresh rosemary
   (dry may be used instead)

1/2 tsp thyme
Garlic powder or fresh minced garlic
Salt and pepper (to taste)
1–1 1/2 cups Island Delight Sweet and
   Sour Sauce (similar sauce okay)

Pre-heat oven to 400°. Cut chicken breasts into halves. Remove skin and visible fat and wash under cold water. Pat dry and drain on paper towels. Dip chicken in egg, making sure chicken is well moistened on both sides. Roll chicken in seasoned crumbs, evenly covering both sides. Heat olive oil in large shallow skillet. Carefully place the chicken pieces into skillet, browning each side evenly, approximately 2–3 minutes per side. Remove chicken from skillet and place in large baking dish which has been sprayed with Pam or similar product. Before placing chicken in oven, sprinkle rosemary, thyme and garlic over the top of chicken. Add salt and pepper to taste. Bake at 400° for 10 minutes. Reduce heat to 350° and pour sweet and sour sauce evenly over the top. Bake for another 15–20 minutes. Don't overcook! This chicken is low in fat and cholesterol. A delicious, healthy dish.

The Crew Cuts
Rudi Maugeri

Paul McCartney was once quoted as saying, "One of the greatest influences in our early careers was The Crew Cuts." He went on to confess, "I was a fan when I was about fourteen or something. I was one of the boys at the stage door of the Empire in Liverpool, waiting for The Crew Cuts to come out. Do you remember them? They covered a lot of hits. They had the hit 'Earth Angel' in England. And they talked to me. They gave me an autograph. They weren't afraid of me."

In 1954, The Crew Cuts were formed in Toronto, Canada. Pat Barrett, Rudi Maugeri and John and Ray Perkins signed with Mercury Records and recorded what many of us think of as the first Rock & Roll hit, "Sh-Boom" (a song that had originally been released as an R & B hit by The Chords). A year later, The Crew Cuts recorded "Earth Angel" and sold another million records.

Today, Rudi Maugeri and his wife of more than 30 years, Marilyn, make their home in Los Angeles and Nevada where they operate their "Fully Alive Centers." Various twelve-step meetings, family and therapy groups as well as private counseling fill their center's daily curriculum. The Maugeris have also written a book entitled *How To Become Fully Alive*. John Perkins resides in New Orleans and writes an entertainment column for the local paper. His brother, Ray, lives in Las Vegas. Pat Barrett lives in Atlantic City and works in real estate.

Sh-Boom Chicken

4 chicken breasts
3/4 cup uncooked rice
1 can (4 oz) mushroom stems and pieces

1 can (10 1/2 oz) cream of mushroom soup
1 envelope onion soup mix
10 1/2 oz milk

Pre-heat oven to 350°. Mix mushroom soup and milk, reserving 1/2 cup of the mixture. Mix remaining soup mixture, rice, mushrooms (with liquid) and half the onion soup mix. Pour into ungreased 11 1/2" x 7 1/2" x 1 1/2" baking dish. Place chicken on top, pour reserved soup mixture over chicken breasts and sprinkle with the remaining onion soup mix. Cover with aluminum foil and bake 1 hour. Uncover and bake 15 minutes longer.

The Crystals
Dee Dee Kenniebrew

The Crystals, one of the early '60s girl groups produced by the legendary Phil Spector, experienced a long career with one hit record after another. Today, Dee Dee Kenniebrew writes us from her home in Atlanta, Georgia: "Little did I know that 'And Then He Kissed Me,' 'He's A Rebel,' 'He's Sure The Boy I Love,' 'There's No Other Like My Baby' and 'Uptown' would etch a lifetime of travel in the form of a singing career that would still be going strong after 30 years!"

As the only original member of The Crystals still "da doo ron ronning" all over the world (the other girls left for marriage and children), Dee Dee sends us her fav-orite recipe: "Da Doo Ron Ron Chicken." The song "Da Doo Ron Ron" was also her personal favorite Crystals hit. She says, "After so many restaurants and hotels I look forward to whipping up some tasty dish when I'm home and have the time."

We enjoyed doing a show with Dee Dee and her Crystals in 1991 at Iron World, U.S.A. Bobby Vee, Dickey Lee and Paul and Paula were also on the show. When The Crystals were singing "He's A Rebel" we all stood in the wings watching and swaying to the music. They were great!

Today, Dee Dee loves living in Atlanta, which is, she says, "a long way from Brooklyn, New York!"

Da Doo Ron Ron Chicken

1 medium chicken, cut into small pieces
1 large onion, finely chopped
Vinegar and oil dressing
Sugar

Garlic powder
Salt and pepper
1 Tbsp tomato paste
1/2 cup water

Pierce and season chicken with salt, pepper, garlic powder and onion. Marinate chicken overnight in dressing and chopped onion. Cover or plastic-bag it. Put a little oil in large skillet, just enough to cover bottom of pan. Dust sugar lightly onto slightly heated oil. Shake off excess marinade before putting chicken into skillet. Add chicken, a few pieces at a time, into skillet. Brown with sugar on both sides, remove them from the pan and set aside. Continue browning all chicken pieces by adding a little sugar to bottom of skillet as needed. When all chicken is brown, add marinade to skillet and add browned chicken. Add a little water and tomato paste. Cover and simmer until chicken is tender. Serve over white rice.

The Drifters
Bobby Hendricks

Before he joined The Drifters, Bobby Hendricks had a group called The Five Crowns and also sang with The Swallows. In 1957, when he replaced Clyde McPhatter as The Drifters' lead singer, he added a whole new dimension to the group, singing lead on "Moonlight Bay" and the classic "Drip Drop." Great Britain was rocking to the incredible sound of The Drifters as Bobby and the group toured there in 1957.

In the summer of 1958, the original Drifters disbanded. But, as we all know, their name lived on to generate many more hits with many other great lead vocalists. Despite those changes, they're probably one of the only groups who spent their entire career on the same record label, Atlantic Records.

In 1958, the same year the original Drifters broke up, Bobby Hendricks and guitar player Jimmy Oliver wrote the classic song "Itchy Twitchy Feelin'," which was released as a Bobby Hendricks single and became a big hit on Sue Records.

Today, Bobby lives with his wife Ruth in Los Angeles. He continues to perform regularly as The Drifters—and they're incredible. We did a show with them in San Diego in December, 1992, and had a fabulous time. Bobby has given us his recipe for "Itchy Twitchy Trinidadian Curried Chicken," but, he says, "Save the last bite for me!"

Itchy Twitchy Trinidadian Curried Chicken (Save The Last Bite For Me)

1 whole chicken, cut up
1/4 cup cooking oil
2 Tbsp West Indian curry
2 Tbsp granulated sugar
1/2 cup onions, chopped
1/2 cup green peppers, chopped
1 tsp black pepper

1 tsp garlic powder
2 tsp seasoned salt
1 tsp poultry seasoning
1/4 cup teriyaki sauce
1 3/4 cups water
2 tsp cornstarch

Season chicken with seasoned salt, black pepper, garlic powder and poultry seasoning. Marinate in teriyaki sauce. Heat cooking oil in large pot. Add sugar and allow it to melt and burn. Sugar will turn dark brown like syrup. Add chicken, turning constantly to allow all pieces to brown. Add curry, stirring frequently. Add onion and green peppers, then 1 1/2 cups water and simmer for 1 hour. Add cornstarch to 1/4 cup water and stir until cornstarch is dissolved. Add cornstarch mixture to chicken and simmer for 15 minutes. This will cause gravy to thicken to the right consistency. Serve over white rice and enjoy!

Lesley Gore

Oscar nominee Lesley Gore (for co-writing "Out Here On My Own" with her brother Michael for the motion picture *Fame*) says, "Yes, there is life after records! But," she jokes, "I don't know if there was life before records."

With over two dozen chart hits to her credit, Lesley helped create "the soundtrack to the '60s" with hits like "Judy's Turn To Cry," "She's A Fool," "That's The Way Boys Are," "You Don't Own Me" and her classic smash hit "It's My Party"—the song that first skyrocketed her to fame in 1963 when she was only sixteen years old. But Brooklyn-born Lesley had already worked as a professional singer before she was discovered by Quincy Jones and signed with Mercury Records.

Unlike many young stars in the '60s, Lesley decided to get her college education while still managing to ex-

perience a recording career. She succeeded, graduating from Sarah Lawrence University with a degree in literature and drama. After graduation, Lesley did that "working five nights a week, month after month" in clubs and lounges while also working as an actress in summer stock productions of *Funny Girl, South Pacific, Finian's Rainbow* and *There's A Girl In My Soup.*

Today, the girl who once wanted to cry at her party is all smiles. She continues to perform, maintaining a first-class career as a concert attraction. Recently, she bought a house in Southhampton, where she hopes to again pursue her very esoteric art of stained-glass sculpture. Lesley continues to compose and has had her songs recorded by artists such as Dusty Springfield, Patti Austin and Bernadette Peters.

It's My Party Chicken

1 whole chicken (3 1/2–4 lb),
   cut into small pieces
1 cup sour cream
2 tsp lemon juice
2 tsp Worcestershire sauce
2 tsp celery salt

1 tsp paprika
2 cloves pressed garlic
Salt and pepper
Cornflake crumbs
Grated Reggiano Parmesan cheese
   (best quality available)

Wash chicken pieces and dry thoroughly on paper towels. In mixing bowl, combine sour cream, lemon juice, Worcestershire sauce, celery salt, salt, paprika, pepper and pressed garlic to make batter. In another bowl, mix together cornflake crumbs and cheese. Dip chicken pieces first in batter, then into crumb mixture. Put in buttered baking dish and place in oven pre-heated to 350° for 50–60 minutes.

Chuck Jackson

There aren't many artists from the '60s who can claim to have had Dionne Warwick as a background singer on their records, but Chuck Jackson can. She can be heard singing with him on his hits "Any Day Now," written by Burt Bacharach, and "I Don't Want To Cry," written by Chuck. He had a total of fifteen chart records between 1961 and 1968, but that was not the end of his success. In 1991, he was nominated for a Grammy in the Best Contemporary Blues Recording category for *Red, Hot And Blue*, an album he did with the late Republican cowboy, Lee Atwater.

Today, Chuck continues to perform. He was seen at Carnegie Hall in New York City as part of the "New York Pops Sixth Anniversary Gala," and his performance during the halftime show at the Sunkist Fiesta Bowl on New Year's Day, 1991, was televised nationally. His recent appearance at the legendary Hollywood Roosevelt Hotel's famed Cinegrill drew a stellar audience that included Dionne Warwick, Burt Bacharach, Henry Mancini and Bruce Springsteen.

When not busy traveling and performing, Chuck enjoys spending time at home in New Jersey with his wife Helen Cash. He is learning to express himself by painting and finds it very relaxing. He's a gourmet chef (wait till you try his favorite recipe, "Any Day Now I'll Make You Chicken In A Dutch Oven"), takes long walks and bicycles at least fifteen miles three times a week.

It was Christmas 1964, when we worked with Chuck at the Brooklyn Fox Theatre in New York. We did five shows a day, starting in the morning and going into the night! Everyone would excitedly watch from the wings when he was on. Chuck was a real inspiration.

Any Day Now I'll Make Roast Chicken In A Dutch Oven

1 whole chicken (3 lb)
26 garlic cloves, whole unpeeled and
   oiled, then washed and towel dried
12 small white onions

4 small new potatoes, unpeeled, washed
   and oiled
2 Tbsp vegetable oil, for potatoes

Wash the chicken and pat dry. Place chicken chest side up in a Dutch oven. Arrange the garlic evenly around the chicken. Layer the onions over the garlic, and place 2 potatoes on each side of the chicken. Tightly cover and place the pot in a cold oven. Heat to 350° and cook covered for 1 hour. (This chicken needs no basting!)

After 1 hour, if the chicken is not brown, leave in the oven uncovered for approximately 10 minutes or longer until browned.

Martha and The Vandellas
Martha Reeves

Martha Reeves (Martha and The Vandellas) first came to Berry Gordy's attention when the group sang background on the Marvin Gaye hits "Stubborn Kind Of Fella," "Hitch Hike" and "Pride And Joy." Martha and The Vandellas' first big hit, "Come And Get These Memories," is often referred to as the beginning of the "Motown Sound." The group went on to have over 21 chart records, including "Heat Wave," "Quicksand," "Dancing In The Street," "I'm Ready For Love," "Jimmy Mack" and "Honey Chile."

Martha was born and raised in Detroit, Michigan, as the eldest of eleven children. She names her parents, Elijah and Ruby Reeves, as her main musical inspirations. They sang and played the guitar for many fun-filled hours of family entertainment.

When she was a young girl, Martha began work as a secretary in the Artist and Repertoire department at Motown Records. She then began performing executive assistant duties for Berry Gordy, Stevie Wonder, Smokey Robinson and Holland-Dozier-Holland. From there, she did some background work as a singer, ultimately landing the Marvin Gaye sessions that launched her career.

Martha is now on the road approximately 42 weeks each year performing throughout the United States and abroad. Along with The Vandellas, her background singers, she has enjoyed over 30 wonderful years of performing. She still lives in Detroit and has attended Lee Strasberg's Theatre Institute in New York. Martha was featured in the film *Fairy Tales* and in an episode of the *Quincy* TV series.

Dancin' In The Street Turkey Sausage Delight

1 pkg smoked turkey sausage
1 (12-oz) pkg curly noodles
1/2 cup tomatoes
1/2 cup onions, chopped
3/4 cup green peppers, chopped

1/2 cup celery, chopped
1 tsp parsley
1 tsp rosemary
1 tsp sage
1 tsp thyme
Salt and pepper

Boil turkey sausage for 5 minutes. Add salt, pepper, sage, rosemary, thyme and parsley, and boil for another 5 minutes. Add noodles, cooking until tender (estimated time: 5 minutes boil and 5 minutes simmer). Add tomatoes, onions, green peppers and celery and simmer 2 minutes. Serve hot with garlic bread, dinner bread, rolls, croissants or whatever works.

Paul and Paula

In 1962, while they were attending Howard Payne University in Brownwood, Texas, Jill Jackson and Ray Hildebrand (later tagged "Paul and Paula") became a singing team. They were invited by a local radio station to sing at a charity show, and the audience response was so overwhelming that they were asked to do a weekly program. It was during this time that Ray ("Paul") wrote the song "Hey Paula." The duo took the song to the Clifford Herring Recording Studio in Fort Worth, Texas, and recorded what would become one of the biggest hits of the '60s.

Phillips Records signed them for national distribution, and in 1962 "Hey Paula" was number one in the nation for fifteen weeks. Paul and Paula received their first gold record on Dick Clark's *American Bandstand*. A platinum record soon followed, which was presented to them when they were touring Great Britain.

Their second hit was called "Young Lovers," and their album, *Paul and Paula Sing For Young Lovers*, was the biggest selling album of 1963.

Although Jill and Ray live in different parts of the country, they continue to perform together doing their rehearsing over the telephone—Ray in Overland Park, Kansas, and Jill in Encino, California.

We do a lot of shows with Paul and Paula, and they're like "family." In fact, we all went for our first visit to The National Music Foundation while performing together in a club near Orlando, Florida.

Hey, Hey Pollo

8 large chicken breasts,
  boned and skinned
8 slices bacon
1 (4 oz) jar chipped beef or dried beef

1 can cream of mushroom soup
  (I use 2 cans)
1 cup sour cream (I use 2 cups)

Line a greased 13" x 9" baking dish with dried beef, covering bottom and sides. Wrap each chicken breast with slice of bacon. Arrange chicken on dried beef. Mix soup and sour cream. Pour mixture over chicken. Bake uncovered at 275° for 3 hours. Serves 8, or 4 hungry folks.

Bobby Rydell

an outstanding drummer, an agile dancer and an extremely fine actor with a true gift for comedy.

In the late '50s and early '60s, Bobby thrilled Rock & Roll audiences with his great hits "Kissin' Time," "We Got Love," "Wild One," "Swingin' School," "Sway," "Volare," "Forget Him" and a list of others. In 1961, he teamed up with Chubby Checker and had a Christmas hit with "Jingle Bell Rock."

Bobby's latest project is a recently completed album including ten songs from the Big Band era. Bobby says, "When I was a little boy of four or five years old, my dad used to take me to the Earl Theatre in Philly to see big band concerts. I fell under the spell of Artie Shaw, Les Brown and Benny Goodman. Now it's time for me to acknowledge how much their music has meant to me through the years in the only way I can." The project, which he describes as "a labor of love," features Bobby backed by a 30-piece orchestra and includes such classics as "Cry Me A River" and "That's All."

Bobby Rydell's career spans several decades and encompasses nearly every area of the entertainment world. From his debut in the '50s as a Rock & Roll teen idol to starring roles in films such as *Bye Bye Birdie* and plays such as *West Side Story* to countless TV appearances throughout the world, Bobby has earned an international reputation as a "classic" performer. Unquestionably a superb singer, he has also proven himself to be

In his spare time, Bobby is a highly vocal and visible fan of the Philadelphia hockey, basketball, football and baseball teams. He and his wife, Camille, live in suburban Philadelphia, close to where he grew up.

Wild One Chicken

4 chicken breasts, quartered
1 large onion, sliced
6 large potatoes, sweet and baking,
   quartered
3 carrots, sliced thick, diagonally
2 cups peas
1/4 lb margarine
1 cup sweet vermouth
Seasonings: salt, pepper, garlic powder,
   basil, oregano and paprika

Line chicken breasts in large baking pan. Add potatoes, carrots and sliced onion. Dot with margarine. Season chicken to taste with all of the above seasonings. Season potatoes with salt, pepper and garlic powder. Cover with foil and bake at 400° for 1 hour. Remove foil and add peas and vermouth. Cook uncovered until chicken is brown on all sides. Serves 6.

Santo and Johnny
Johnny Farina

Johnny Farina is the younger brother of the Santo and Johnny duo. The two siblings wrote a song called "Sleepwalk" in 1959 when Santo was 22 and Johnny was only 18. That same year, it became one of the biggest hits of the summer, sending chills up and down the spines of everyone who heard it. Later, the song would be heard by Neil Armstrong in his helmet as he made the first walk on the moon. "Sleepwalk" has also earned the duo BMI's "Million Air Award" for one million radio airplays of the song in the United States alone and was featured in the movie, *La Bamba*.

Santo and Johnny recorded for Canadian American Records from 1959 to 1964 and, though their other records were never as big as "Sleepwalk," they still had several other substantial hits including "Tear Drop," "Caravan" and "Twistin' Bells." During the late '50s and early '60s they toured around the world and were particularly successful in Europe. They also appeared on all the popular TV shows of the day including Dick Clark's *American Bandstand* and Alan Freed's *The Big Beat*.

Johnny continues to write and perform. In 1989, we did the "Legends of Rock & Roll" show with Santo and Johnny at the Greek Theatre in Los Angeles and watched from the wings as they thrilled the audience. They've also done several shows to benefit The National Music Foundation.

Sleepwalk To The Kitchen And Try Some Garlic Chicken

1 broiler chicken (3 lb), cut up
3 cloves garlic, minced
4 sprigs parsley, minced
1 pinch oregano

1/2 tsp pepper
Oil
1 lb linguini

Cover bottom of 5-quart pot with oil, about 1/8" deep, and brown garlic. Add parsley, oregano and pepper. Then add chicken and brown until skin is golden in color (about 10 minutes). Add enough water to cover chicken (about 4 cups). Let it cook slowly for about 45 minutes. Boil linguine (al dente). Drain and place in a large serving platter. Pour the chicken juice over the linguine, then place the chicken on the pasta. Serve and enjoy.

Neil Sedaka

In the early '60s, the "Brill Building" writers in New York City could take credit for the majority of the Top 40 songs on the pop charts. Neil Sedaka was one of these writers, and included in the countdown were numerous Sedaka classics, among them "Stupid Cupid" and "Where The Boys Are" (recorded by Connie Francis) and his own vocal hits such as "Calendar Girl," "Oh! Carol," "Stairway To Heaven," "Next Door To An Angel," "Happy Birthday Sweet Sixteen" and "Breaking Up Is Hard To Do." Between 1959 and 1963, over 25 million Neil Sedaka records were sold.

As the author of more than one thousand songs, Neil has been inducted into the Songwriter's Hall of Fame. In 1975, his song "Laughter In The Rain" was a number-one single, but his composition of "Love Will Keep Us Together," the song that launched the career of The Captain and Tenille, won a Grammy for Record Of The Year. Then came "Bad Blood" and a remake of his 1962 smash "Breaking Up Is Hard To Do."

An alumnus of the prestigious Juilliard School of Music, Neil continues to perform throughout the world. His enormously popular sell-out concert appearances, as well as his engagements in Atlantic City, Las Vegas and Reno, continue to earn him exceptional reviews.

Neil has written his autobiography entitled *Laughter In The Rain*, and is currently working on a two-hour TV film based on his meeting and courtship with his wife, Leba, from 1958 through 1962, and the songs Neil recorded during that time.

Breakin' Up Is Hard To Do—But Making Mary's Voo Doo Chicken Is Easy

1 whole chicken (2 1/2–3 lb),
   cut into serving pieces
2 cups white vinegar
2 Tbsp soy sauce
1 large onion, sliced

4 cloves garlic, peeled but left whole
1/2 tsp black pepper
4 Tbsp Dijon mustard
6 Tbsp ketchup
2 Tbsp milk

Marinate chicken for several hours in combined vinegar, soy sauce, onion, garlic and pepper. Drain, reserving liquid. Combine mustard with 4 Tbsp ketchup and dip each piece of chicken into this mixture, coating well. Bake chicken, skin side down, at 350° for 30 minutes. Turn pieces, and pour remaining ketchup— mixed with milk and reserved marinade— over chicken. Bake an additional 45 minutes. Serve with white rice. Serves 4.

Dodie Stevens

At age sixteen, with her career at its peak, Dodie left show business and got married. The marriage lasted only five years, long enough to produce a daughter, Stephanie. After her divorce, Dodie tried to return to a singing career but found the music industry had drastically changed. Trying to differentiate her image from "cute little Dodie Stevens," she used her real name, Geri, and joined Sergio Mendes And Brazil 1977. She stayed with the group for one year, leaving to work as a background singer for Loretta Lynn, Boz Skaggs, Harry Belafonte and Diahann Carroll. Then, for twelve years, she worked exclusively for Mac Davis as a singer/dancer.

Today, Geri lives in the San Fernando Valley in California and is currently touring with The Golden Boys—Frankie Avalon, Fabian and Bobby Rydell. She and daughter Stephanie are also singing as a duo. Their sound encompasses the heart and rhythm of Country & Western, but with the soul of rock and blues. Much of their repertoire is their own original material. As Dodie Stevens, she can also be found singing "Pink Shoelaces" on the Rock & Roll revival circuit.

Dodie Stevens (born Geraldine Ann Pasquale) was a singing prodigy at the age of four. By the time she was seven, she began making local TV appearances and in 1959, at the age of thirteen, had a number-one hit record called "Pink Shoelaces." Her career skyrocketed and she appeared on all the popular TV variety shows of the day. She even starred with Fabian in her first film, *Hound Dog Man*.

Doolie's Divine Chicken Thighs

8 chicken thighs
2 Tbsp butter
2 Tbsp safflower oil
Spike seasoning

Garlic powder
Onion powder
Pepper
1 cup water

Melt butter and safflower oil in skillet. Rub spices on chicken thighs and brown on each side (approximately 2–3 minutes per side). Add water, cover and simmer for 35–45 minutes. During cooking, you may need to add more water if it evaporates too quickly. You may add potatoes and/or other vegetables—seasoned with same spices—after you add the water, if desired.

Yes
Tony Kaye and Alan White

They were perhaps the last supergroup to blast out of London's Marquee Club. In all its various incarnations, Yes has set out to prove to the world that rock music can be taken seriously. Singer Jon Anderson and bassist Chris Squire believed that the raw power and excitement of Rock & Roll, if blended with the complexities and rich textures of classical music and the fluid risk-taking of jazz, could produce something magical. Labeled "Britain's Brightest Hope of 1969," Yes pioneered what would be called "Progressive" or "Art Rock" in the late '60s. Their third recording, *The Yes Album* launched them into international fame, introducing such classics as "I've Seen All Good People," "Yours Is No Disgrace" and "Starship Trooper."

In 1972, Jon Anderson and Steve Howe penned a tune called "Roundabout," which became a Yes trademark—it was everything they aspired to, showcasing the band's individual and collective strengths.

After nine hugely successful albums and ten years on the road, Yes took a breather, reuniting in 1982 to record *90125* (named after the album's catalogue number) which included their only single to reach the top of the charts, "Owner of a Lonely Heart," penned by Yes newcomer Trevor Rabin. They have since released four more albums, including the recent *Union*, which has captured the hearts of old fans as well as bringing in legions of new ones.

We have two Yes recipes—from drummer Alan White and keyboardist Tony Kaye.

Shepherd's Pie A La Chalky

8 lbs potatoes, peeled and mashed
6 lbs breast of turkey, minced
2 onions
2 lbs carrots, peeled and sliced
1 2-lb bag frozen peas

2 tsp Spike (mixed spices)
2 tsp Worcestershire sauce
1/2 cup gravy mix
2 or 3 tomatoes
1 lb cheddar cheese, shredded

Cook the minced turkey and onions with half of the Spike and half of the Worcestershire sauce until tender and golden brown. Place in bottom of a pie dish. Make gravy and add half to turkey mixture. Layer carrots on top along with frozen peas. Cook and mash potatoes, then spread over top of pie. Arrange the tomatoes in a pattern on top of the mashed potatoes. Sprinkle with cheese and add remaining Spike and Worcestershire sauce. Bake at 350° for 30 minutes or until cheese has melted, then brown under the broiler. Serve with the remainder of the gravy. Serves 8–10.

Miss Holly's Rebel Chicken

6 chicken breasts
Salt and pepper
Garlic
Lemon juice
Olive oil

Butter
Durkees Famous Sauce
    (made of corn oil, vinegar,
    water, sugar, spices, salt,
    eggs, cornstarch)

Pre-heat oven to 375°. Wash chicken. and marinate in salt, pepper, garlic, lemon juice, olive oil and butter. Bake on sheet pan, covered with foil for 35 minutes. Remove from oven and pour excess juice into a bowl. Cover chicken with Durkees Famous Sauce. Pour excess juice from bowl over chicken. Bake uncovered for 35 minutes or until done. Serve with mashed potatoes and green vegetable (cabbage or green beans are great cooked with bacon on simmer).

The Collector's Page

OTIS REDDING

For information on how to order this Rock 'n' Roll/ Rhythm and Blues Commemorative Stamp, please see page 2.

6
Meat Entrees

Deep Purple Italian Special

Daddy G's New Orleans Delight

Roly Poly Meatballs (With A Peppermint Twist?)

Come Go With Me For Curry Goat Gumbo

Iko Iko Dixie Meat Sauce

Bye Bye Love Chili

Come Softly To Me And Taste This Ground Steak

The Pineapple Princess' Peanut Butter Pork Chops

Hammer Slip Bone Ribs

Itsy Bitsy Teenie Weenies With Yellow Peppers And Zucchinis

Dead Man's Curve Spaghetti Pie

Merry-Go-Round Steak's Got What It Takes

**I Was Tossin' And Turnin' All Night
Thinkin' About Stuffed Calves Hearts**

Good Golly, It's Southern Homemade Brunswick Stew

Lady Godiva's Spaghetti Carbonara

Hal's Neckbones Supreme

Pie And Mash

Mashed Potato Shepherd's Pie And Gravy

Sixteen Reasons Why You'll Love My Italian Meat Sauce

Oogum Boogum Lite Chili

Burnt Weenie Sandwich

April Stevens and Nino Tempo

By early 1962, April Stevens and Nino Tempo (a brother-sister team from Niagara Falls, New York) had perfected "a sound." They signed with ATCO Records, and struck gold with their first release, "Sweet and Lovely." In the autumn of 1963 they burned up the airwaves with their Grammy Award-winning interpretation of "Deep Purple." April came up with the idea to record the song and Nino did the arrangement. "Nino was supposed to sing the second chorus by himself," explains April. "He didn't know the words, so I started speaking them to him." A friend who heard the demo thought April's "narration" sounded great. They went into the studio to record another song, and with fourteen minutes of studio time left decided to try "Deep Purple." Says Nino, "We talked about it for 30 seconds, then recorded it. In fourteen minutes we got two takes." Nino called Ahmet Ertegun of Atlantic Records in New York and said, "We're sending the master of 'Deep Purple' just the way it is. It's a hit!" Two weeks passed and Ahmet didn't return the call. Finally, Nino telephoned and asked him what he thought. Ahmet said it was the most embarrassing thing April and Nino had ever recorded and it went on the shelf. "Paradise" was released, but it didn't make the Hot 100. "I called Ahmet and asked for our contract back," Nino recalls. "He told me, 'I'll release one more record, and if it flops, you've got your contract back.'" Nino wanted to sign with his friend Phil Spector, who also thought "Deep Purple" could be big. Ahmet released "Deep Purple" and the rest is history.

Today, 30 years later, Nino Tempo has again signed with Ahmet Ertegun on Atlantic—this time as a jazz sax artist. April is singing on one of the cuts on his latest album, *Nino*. Nino now lives in Beverly Hills, and April and her husband are in the process of moving from Southern California to Scottsdale, Arizona.

Deep Purple Italian Special

2 lbs lean ground chuck
2 boxes frozen chopped spinach, cooked
1 box mushrooms, chopped
3/4 large onion, chopped
2 cloves garlic, chopped
4 eggs

4 Tbsp soy sauce
Salt, pepper, lemon pepper and
  Italian seasoning (to taste)
Olive oil (to cover bottom of frying pan
  or wok)

Mix ground meat, onion, garlic, mushrooms, soy sauce and seasoning together in large bowl. Put oil in pan over medium fire. Add meat mixture to pan, stirring until brown. Add spinach and lower flame slightly. Keep stirring until all is cooked (about 3 minutes). Add eggs and mix all together in pan until eggs are firm, or however you like them. Put on plate and add Parmesan cheese. *Bon appétit!* Serves 4.

Gary "U.S." Bonds

When his first hit record was released—a song we all remember, called "New Orleans"—promotional copies were sent to various radio stations in record sleeves inscribed "Buy U.S. Bonds." Hence Gary Anderson, age nineteen, became Gary "U.S." Bonds.

The follow-up to "New Orleans" was the now-legendary party record entitled "Quarter To Three." It was originally an instrumental called "A Night With Daddy G" when Gary and Gene "Daddy G" Barge went on to write and arrange what became

a number-one hit that would eventually inspire Bruce Springsteen to say of Gary, "There's some guys out there, what they do is forever."

Gary went on to have numerous chart records over the next several years including "School Is Out," "Dear Lady Twist" and "Twist, Twist Señora." He is heard performing his classic hits in such films as *D.C. Cab*, *Class Reunion*, *Mask*, *Children Of The Corn* and *Beetlejuice*.

Although he performs all over the world, Gary continues to write songs for other artists. He was nominated for a Grammy for writing a number-one country hit for the great Johnny Paycheck. The song, "Friend, Don't Take Her She's All I've Got," also earned Gary the nomination for the Country Music Association's Songwriter of the Year. The song also became a number-one R & B hit for Freddie North.

We have a lot of fond memories of Gary, going back to the first Gary "U.S." Bonds tour in 1961 and, as current as 1990, when we did a sold-out concert in Sarasota, Florida, to benefit The National Music Foundation. And isn't it a small world? We wrote "Let's Have A Hand For The Little Lady" for Johnny Paycheck. Old Rock & Rollers never die—they just start writing country music!

Daddy G's New Orleans Delight

3–4 pieces chicken
1 lb shrimp, cleaned
2 cans crabmeat
2 cups oysters
1 lb smoked sausage
1 large onion, chopped
2 cloves garlic, minced

1 pkg frozen okra
1 can (28 oz) whole tomatoes
1 Tbsp flour
2 bay leaves
Salt and pepper
Old bay seasoning

Place chicken and sausage in water and boil until chicken is tender. Remove bones and cut up chicken and sausage. Save broth. In large pot, sauté onions and garlic in shortening. Add flour and blend. Add tomatoes, broth, okra and simmer 15 minutes. Add all remaining ingredients and cook 1 hour (should be thick). Serve over cooked rice.

Joey Dee and The Starliters
Joey Dee

In 1961, New York City came alive! Every night, a club on 45th Street played host to New York's elite. This club became known throughout the world as "The Peppermint Lounge," and Joey Dee was the man singing "The Peppermint Twist." Written by Joey along with Henry Glover, the song became a major hit on Roulette Records and was followed with many other hits for Joey, including "Hey, Let's Twist," "Shout," "What Kind Of Love Is This" and others. And guess where Joey met and fell in love with his wife, Lois Lee. That's right—"The Peppermint Lounge."

The National Music Foundation is a reality today because of a dream that Joey Dee had several years ago. Deeply affected by Jackie Wilson's tragic death (he died penniless after being in a coma for an extended period of time), Joey decided it was time that the music business started "taking care of their own." He founded The Foundation For The Love Of Rock & Roll, which has now expanded its horizons to include musicians of every stripe and has become The National Music Foundation.

During the past few years, Joey has made appearances on several TV shows to share his dream and awaken people to the needs that exist in the music industry. People became aware of the goals of The National Music Foundation from shows such as *Sally Jesse Raphael*, *The Everyday Show With Joan Lunden*, *Good Morning America*, *20/20* and *The CBS Morning Show*.

Today, Joey and Lois live in Clearwater, Florida, and continue to perform as Joey Dee and The Starliters. Their son, Ronnie, is a member of the band, singing and playing sax. The entire Dee family is actively involved with The National Music Foundation, and they do shows regularly to benefit this worthy organization.

Roly Poly Meatballs (With A Peppermint Twist?)

1 lb ground chuck
1/2 cup Italian seasoned bread crumbs
1 egg
3/4 cup olive oil

1 tsp grated Parmesan cheese
1 Tbsp milk
Salt and pepper

With hands, mix together all ingredients (except oil) while doing the "Peppermint Twist." Form into golf-ball-sized balls. Continue doing the "Peppermint Twist" while you heat olive oil in frying pan. Brown meat balls until deep golden brown. (Add oil as needed.) Remove from oil and add to your spaghetti sauce to finish cooking. Continue doing the "Peppermint Twist" while serving.

The Del-Vikings
Norman Wright

One of Rock & Roll's first racially integrated bands, The Del-Vikings are a vocal group that originated at a Pittsburgh Air Force Base back in 1956. "Come Go With Me" was written by Clarence Quick in a (pardon the pun) quick five minutes. The group recorded the song in a friend's basement and made a deal with Fee-Bee Records in Pittsburgh. It was on its way to becoming an instant smash when, a short time later, Dot Records picked up the master. The song became a monster hit on its new label with Norman Wright singing the lead. Other major hits by The Del-Vikings include "Whispering Bells" (also on Dot Records) and "Cool Shake" and "Sunday Kind Of Love" on Mercury Records. They also recorded several albums, including The Best Of The Del-Vikings on Dot and *They Sing, They Swing...The Del-Vikings* on Mercury.

The Del-Vikings can be heard singing "Come Go With Me" and "Whispering Bells" in the hit movie *Stand By Me*. "Come Go With Me" was also used in the movie *American Graffiti* and, more recently, in *Joe Versus The Volcano*.

Today, The Del-Vikings perform worldwide in major clubs, in concert, on TV specials, in Las Vegas and Atlantic City, Radio City Music Hall in New York and the Universal Amphitheatre and the Greek Theatre in Los Angeles. Their hits have been re-recorded digitally, and their albums are available on CD's, LP's and cassettes presently being distributed nationally through major record-store chains.

Come Go With Me For Curry Goat Gumbo

2 lbs goat meat, chopped
1/4 cup vinegar
2 tsp lemon juice
3 bay leaves
Thyme, dash
Ground cloves, dash
Peppercorn (to taste)
Crushed red peppers (optional)

Marinate goat meat overnight with above ingredients. In a 3-qt pot, add 2 qts water to the above. Then add:

1/2 lb fresh baby okra
2 young carrots
3 stalks young celery
1 small can stewed tomatoes (drained)
1 small can baby lima beans (drained)
1 small can whole kernel corn (drained)
1 medium onion, chopped/diced

Cook until done. Serve on bed of brown wild rice with corn bread (try the B-52's, Mel Carter's or Linda Ronstadt's) or corn fritters.

The Dixie Cups
Barbara Hawkins and Rosa Lee Hawkins

Sisters and founding Dixie Cups, Rosa and Barbara Hawkins, still live in their hometown of New Orleans, Louisiana. Their record, "Chapel Of Love," sold millions and was number one for three weeks in 1964, making them the only American girl group to knock The Beatles out of the top spot on the charts. The record received national attention again recently, when it was a featured song on the soundtrack album for the film *The Big Easy*.

The Dixie Cups have not stopped performing since "Chapel Of Love" back in 1964.

Their next big hit was "Iko Iko" in 1965, followed by several best-selling albums. "Ninety-nine percent of our work is around the world," says Rosa. "As with all New Orleans entertainers, we'd love to perform more at home. But we've spent the last two summers in Italy, Switzerland and Germany." The Hawkins sisters were joined by Ms. Dale Mickle many years ago, when she replaced third original member Joan Johnson, who dropped out of the group in 1966 when she learned she was suffering from sickle-cell anemia.

In 1965, The Dixie Cups were the only black female entertainers that went to Vietnam. They will always remember spending New Year's Eve there when 1966 rolled in.

When not on the road, Rosa and Barbara Hawkins keep busy doing a lot of community service in their beloved New Orleans. They volunteer for United Way and, along with singer Irma Thomas, visit patients in the AIDS Unit of Charity Hospital. Rosa has one son who, in 1991, was the Outstanding College Student of America while attending Florida State University. Barbara has a seven-year-old daughter.

Iko Iko Dixie Meat Sauce

2 lbs chuck (optional) ground
   beef
1 large onion
6 cloves garlic
1 bunch green onions (shallots)
1 bunch parsley
1 Tbsp sugar
1/2 tsp oregano

1 1/2 tsp Italian seasoning
1 large can tomatoes
1 large can tomato paste
Tony's Creole Unsalted Seasoning
1/4 cup red cooking wine
Salt and white pepper
6 large mushrooms, chopped

Chop all seasoning well. Brown the beef in a large deep pot. Remove beef and drain oil from beef and pot. Do not wash pot. Brown seasoning and add meat and all other ingredients to seasoning. Simmer on medium to low heat for 45 minutes. Serves 6–8.

The Everly Brothers
Phil Everly

The Everly Brothers, Don and Phil, were raised in a musical family in the coal-mining towns of Kentucky. Their parents, Ike and Margaret Everly, like their parents before them, were folk and country singers from central Kentucky.

In 1953, the family moved to Knoxville, Tennessee, where they worked on radio station WROL performing two shows a day. Then a decision was made to split up the family act and send the Everly boys to "Music City." Don and Phil suffered repeated rejections by record executives who didn't know what to do with them. But finally, in 1957, they signed with Cadence Records and released "Bye, Bye Love" which sold over two million records.

After "Bye, Bye Love," the brothers turned out an incredible string of classic records, often having several on the charts at the same time. Their phenomenal output over the next five years included "I Wonder If You Care As Much," "Claudette," "Bird Dog," "Devoted To You," "Problems," "Take A Message To Mary," "Till I Kissed You," "Let It Be Me," "When Will I Be Loved" (written by Phil and later a big hit for Linda Ronstadt), "Cathy's Clown," "Wake Up Little Susie," "All I Have To Do Is Dream," "Walk Right Back," "Ebony Eyes" and many, many more.

In 1988, Don and Phil were inducted into the Rock & Roll Hall Of Fame, and the 1990s find them still in demand every-where. They tour six to eight months a year all over the world. But each summer they interrupt their touring schedule to return to their hometown to give a benefit performance—The Everly Brothers Homecoming Music Festival—for the economically depressed coal mining community in Muhlenberg County, Kentucky.

Bye Bye Love Chili (From Phil's Mythical Cookbook On Canular Cuisine)

2 cans Dennison's chili, hot
1 can sweet creamed corn
4 heaping Tbsp La Victoria
   Salsa Ranchero

Mix above ingredients into large saucepan. Heat. Eat. And it's bye-bye love!

The Fleetwoods
Gretchen Christopher

When she was eighteen years old, Gretchen Christopher sat down at the piano at Olympia High School in Olympia, Washington, and composed "Come Softly To Me" to perform at the Senior Class Talent Show. She got together with two classmates, Gary Troxel and Barbara Ellis, and with their street corner humming and harmonies they formed a trio that would become The Fleetwoods. They recorded the song a cappella at home, and Gretchen took the tape to a record promoter in Seattle. "It'll sell a million!" Bob Reisdorff shouted, and he formed Dolphin (Dolton) Records. "Come Softly To Me" became a number-one hit and the first-million seller ever produced in the Northwest. The Fleetwoods went on to achieve ten chart records that included such major hits as "Graduation's Here," "Mr. Blue," "Tragedy" and "The Great Imposter."

In 1985, Gretchen toured the Soviet Union and personally distributed goodwill gift cassettes of *The Fleetwoods Greatest Hits* behind the Iron Curtain. The group has performed their hits from Finland to Russia to Mexico. In 1990, their fourteenth album, *The Best Of The Fleetwoods*, was released on CD.

Today, Gretchen, a Northwest Music Hall of Fame Inductee and a BMI Million Air Songwriter, divides her time between Washington and California. She still performs with her Fleetwoods and continues to compose, dance and write. Gretchen, who is a "leap year baby," still feels lucky. We keep reminding her that, in reality, she only turned thirteen in 1992!

Come Softly To Me And Taste This Ground Steak

1 lb lean ground beef
4 slices natural cheddar cheese
4 dill pickles, sliced lengthwise

Low or nonfat yogurt
(enough to cover generously)
4 cherry tomatoes

Flatten ground beef, about 1/2" thick, across bottom of steak platter (a frying pan or other bake-and-serve container will do). Place under broiler and broil at 500° until fat is released and beef is medium-well. Pour off fat. Immediately cover beef with slices of cheddar cheese (other natural cheeses may be substituted, including Pepper Jack). Replace under broiler, just long enough to melt cheese and bring meat to doneness. Remove from broiler and immediately cover with a layer of dill pickle slices (or salsa, for variation) and a layer of yogurt. Garnish with cherry tomatoes in center (or 1 for each serving, if pre-dishing plates.) Place steak platter on wooden holder, with spatula for cutting, and perhaps a spoon for drippings, and serve! Variation: After draining meat, ring platter with cherry tomatoes, then cover all with cheese and broil until cheese is melted.

Serving suggestions: Precede with tossed green salad. Serve with whole wheat or sour dough bread to absorb meat/cheese/yogurt drippings. Refresh with orange, tomato or other citrus juice. Follow with slow dancing to "Come Softly To Me."

Annette Funicello

Many people probably don't know it, but it was Annette's record of "Tall Paul" that inspired Ray Hildebrand (Paul and Paula) to write "Hey, Paula." (And we got that straight from the horse's mouth.) "Tall Paul" was an amazing hit and began a whole new career for Annette as a recording artist in 1959.

Born in Utica, New York, Annette was the eldest of three children. Her father, an

automobile mechanic, decided on a whim to move his family to California where he thought he might find better working conditions and a climate more suitable to working outdoors. Much to the family's surprise, their move to California would give America one of its most familiar faces.

At age twelve, Annette was dancing the lead in Swan Lake for her school's recital. She'd been taking dance lessons, and ballet came naturally to her. During one of the performances, without making his presence known, Walt Disney was in the audience. He was scouting talent for a new TV show he was preparing, *The Mickey Mouse Club*. After three callbacks, Annette was chosen as the last of the 24 original Mouseketeers. The show aired from 1955 to 1958.

In 1959, her musical conductor developed a unique "Annette Sound," which led to her first big hit record, "Tall Paul." Her recording career included ten chart records including "First Name Initial," "O Dio Mio" and "Pineapple Princess." She released a total of 24 albums, including a greatest hits album in 1984.

From 1963 through 1966, while on loan to American International, Annette and Frankie Avalon made a total of eight "Beach Party" movies, and 21 years later they appeared together in *Back To The Beach* for Paramount Studios.

In 1989 and 1990, Annette and Frankie reunited to perform live throughout the country with the Frankie and Annette Live concert extravaganza.

The Pineapple Princess' Peanut Butter Pork Chops

6 pork chops, 3/4" thick
1 envelope dry mushroom soup mix
3/4 cup peanut butter, chunky

2 cups water
1 onion, sliced
1/2 green pepper, sliced (optional)

Brown pork chops in oil and remove to another plate. Stir peanut butter and soup mix into drippings while gradually adding water. Bring to boil, reduce heat. Add pork chops, onion, and green pepper. Cover and simmer for 45–50 minutes or until tender. I recommend serving over noodles or rice.

Hammer

"A long time ago, I made the commitment to dedicate at least one song per album to God," explains Hammer. "He has been very good to me, and never for one minute do I want Him to think I've forgotten, because I haven't. I don't care about the commercial success of these songs, just about their spiritual success. I enjoy making songs like 'Pray,' which I never dreamed would become a Top 40 hit. That took me by surprise."

Achieving monumental goals in only a few years, the Oakland, California, native known simply as Hammer was the best-selling and most acclaimed artist of 1990-91, and the most accomplished rap artist in history. His musical and multi-media innovations single-handedly brought hip-hop to the masses, and his theme song, "U Can't Touch This," has become a worldwide anthem. No one can come close to touching Hammer's combination of positivity, aura, spirit, potent sense of style, rhythmic hooks, musical variance, high-voltage choreography and thought-provoking, socially-conscious lyrics.

Before he got started making music, Hammer excelled in a different sort of hit making: baseball. Born Stanley Kirk Burrell in a tough East Oakland neighborhood, one of six children, his first passions were dancing and baseball. At the age of eleven, both interests took him to the Oakland Stadium parking lot where he'd practice James Brown splits, hoping for comp tickets from amused Oakland Athletic's players. Taking notice of his initiative, A's owner Charley Finley gave him a job in the front office and as a batboy. Working at the stadium gave him his first taste of celebrity life—and his nickname. Milwaukee Brewer Pedro Garcia noticed young Stanley's resemblance to "Hammerin'" Hank Aaron. "Then Reggie Jackson started calling me 'Hammer,'" he recalls, "and it's been my name ever since!"

Hammer Slip Bone Ribs

6 lbs beef ribs
1/2 cup ground pepper
1/2 cup seasoned salt
1 cup vinegar

Place ribs in a plastic bag with ground pepper, season salt and vinegar and refrigerate for 24 hours.

Barbeque ribs on a grill filled with mesquite chips and charcoals for 30–40 minutes. Cover barbeque to smoke the meat, and when the fire rises use beer (your choice) to cool down the meat and fire. The secret sauce is in the next edition (meanwhile, try Johnny Tillotson's or Bobby Vee's barbeque sauce). Makes 6 servings.

Marinade can also be used for chicken and pork ribs.

Brian Hyland

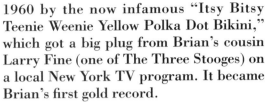

A native of New York City, Brian formed a harmony group called The Delfies in 1959. They cut a demo and made the rounds of the New York record labels. Finally, after much persistence, Brian was signed as a solo artist to a management contract, where he cut demos for band leader Sammy Kaye's publishing company. KAPP Records heard a demo they liked and signed Brian when he was only sixteen years old. His first record, "Rosemary," was followed in the summer of

1960 by the now infamous "Itsy Bitsy Teenie Weenie Yellow Polka Dot Bikini," which got a big plug from Brian's cousin Larry Fine (one of The Three Stooges) on a local New York TV program. It became Brian's first gold record.

Over the years, Brian had a total of 22 "Hot 100" chart records with such hits as "Ginny Come Lately," "Sealed With A Kiss," "The Joker Went Wild" and "Gypsy Woman."

In 1987, after 28 years, Brian was happy to see Rhino Records compile and release the first and only *Brian Hyland's Greatest Hits* on LP and cassette, which includes 14 of his 22 chart singles.

Today, he and his wife Rosemarie live in Helendale, California. Brian continues to perform on a regular basis with son, Bodi, as his drummer and "Ro" playing other percussion instruments. They've traveled all over the world performing Brian's memorable hit songs. In their spare time, they continue to write new music and record and are also compiling material for a book about the *Long and Winding Rock n Roll Road*. (We wonder if they'll mention the "Tour From Hell" we were on with them in 1988.)

Itsy Bitsy Teenie Weenies With Yellow Peppers And Zucchinis

1 lb of your favorite weenies
1 medium onion, cut into 1" pieces
1 yellow pepper, cut into 1" pieces
1 med zucchini, cut into 1" pieces
2 Tbsp olive oil

Pita bread, cut into halves and heated on
   grill
Optional fixin's: Mustard, ketchup, salad
   dressing, pickle relish, steak sauce, hot
   pepper sauce, chili, salsa, yellow pep-
   peroncinis

Heat up the barbie! Cut weenies into
1" pieces, alternate with veggies on skewers. Brush veggies with olive oil. Place
skewers on oiled grill 4"–6" from heat.
Turn and brush with oil several times till
the weenies are brown and bubbly and
the veggies crisp and tender (about 8–10
minutes). Serve in pita halves for everyone to choose their fixin's. Serves 2...
3...4...guess there isn't anymore!

Jan & Dean
Dean Torrance

It might be a surprise to some, but Dean Torrance of Jan and Dean has been nominated three times for a Grammy Award—not for singing, but for designing the Album Cover of the Year. His first nomination came in 1971 for *Uncle Charlie* by The Nitty Gritty Dirt Band. Then, in 1972, Dean won the Grammy for *Polution* by Polution and in 1975, he was nominated again for *Dream* by The Nitty Gritty Dirt Band. Quite a versatile guy!

Dean was not Jan's first singing partner, but was certainly his most successful. In 1958, while still a high school student, Jan was recording with Arnie Ginsberg singing as "Jan and Arnie." They cut a song in Jan's garage called "Jenny Lee," and it became a hit for the duo. Then Arnie got involved with the real Jenny Lee and joined the Navy. Jan decided to contact Dean Torrance to see if he was interested in doing some recording. Since Dean had been singing on "Jenny Lee" along with Jan and Arnie (before doing a six month stint in the Army), and had always felt his name should have been on the label,

he was ready to begin a singing career. Jan acquired a song called "Baby Talk" and the guys worked on it for about two months. They say it took so long because they kept taking breaks to play volleyball, go to the beach or cruise the local drive-in restaurant. Perhaps they might have finished it up a little faster had they known what a monster hit it was to become. "Baby Talk" was their first of 23 chart records, including "Dead Man's Curve."

Dean has sent us his recipe for "Dead Man's Curve Spaghetti Pie." He says, "This is one bitchin' pie—hope you like it as much as I."

Dead Man's Curve Spaghetti Pie

6 oz thin spaghetti (3–4 cups cooked)
2 Tbsp butter
1/2 cup grated Parmesan cheese
2 eggs, well beaten
1 1/2 cups part-skim ricotta cheese
1 lb lean ground beef
3/4 cup onion, chopped

1 can (8 oz) tomatoes, cut up
1 can (6 oz) tomato paste
1 tsp brown sugar
1 tsp oregano
2 cloves garlic, peeled and chopped
3/4 cup shredded low-fat mozzarella
    cheese

Cook spaghetti, drain and turn into 10" pie plate. Stir butter into spaghetti until melted. Add Parmesan cheese and eggs. Toss until spaghetti is evenly coated. Using fingers, shape spaghetti mixture into a "crust," covering sides and bottom of pie plate. Spoon ricotta cheese into spaghetti crust. Spread evenly over bottom. In skillet, brown ground beef with onion and garlic. Drain off excess fat. Stir in undrained tomatoes, tomato paste, sugar and oregano. Heat through until tomato paste deepens in color. Spoon meat mixture into spaghetti crust on top of ricotta cheese. Bake uncovered at 350° for 20 minutes. Sprinkle mozzarella cheese on top. Bake 5 minutes longer, or until cheese melts. Cool slightly. Slice like pie and serve with a crisp green salad and garlic bread.

Marv Johnson

Motown's first international recording artist, Marv Johnson signed with the Motown Record Corporation via the Tamla label in 1958. He was known as "Marvelous Marv Johnson" and led the first Motown Revue with Smokey Robinson and The Miracles, Martha and The Vandellas and Mary Wells.

Marv began his musical career in the 1950s, traveling in carnival shows with his quartet known as The Junior Serenaders. After several years on the "circuit," he accepted the managerial and creative guidance of Berry Gordy, Jr., who at the time was known primarily for his songwriting successes—"Lonely Teardrops" and "To Be Loved" for the legendary Jackie Wilson. Motown was in its infancy, so Marv and Berry joined United Artist Record Company for better, more expansive distribution of Marv's records. What followed was an impressive list of hits including "I Love The Way You Love," "You've Got What It Takes" and "Merry-Go-Round."

During his incredibly successful recording career, Marv toured with the best of them, doing one-nighters with Ray Charles, Sam Cooke, Jackie Wilson, Ruth Brown, Etta James and many other musical greats.

We were sad to learn that Marv Johnson passed away on May 14, 1993. He collapsed while performing on stage at the age of 54. Prior to his sudden death, Marv made his home in Detroit, where he was born and raised, and continued to perform his wonderful hits throughout the United States, Europe and Australia. He will be greatly missed.

Merry-Go-Round Steak's Got What It Takes

1 tender round steak
4 medium sized potatoes, peeled
   and quartered
4 large carrots, peeled and halved
Black pepper

Garlic salt
Seasoned salt
1 large onion, peeled and sliced
1/2 cup water
2 tsp vegetable oil

Beat both sides of steak with a steak mallet. Season both sides with garlic salt, pepper and seasoning salt. Place in broiler pan with water and oil. Surround steak with potatoes and carrots. Place onion rings on top of steak. Cook at 400° until done. Serve.

Bobby Lewis

Bobby Lewis began his career in the early '60s when he toured with Jackie Wilson and James Brown as their Master of

Ceremonies. Then, in 1961, Bobby's dream came true—he had his very own hit record with "Tossin' And Turnin'" More than just a hit, this was the biggest selling record of the year in 1961. In 1976, *Billboard* magazine named "Tossin' And Turnin' " as the fifth most popular and best-selling hit in Rock & Roll history. His follow-up, "One Track Mind," was also a smash.

During the '60s, Bobby worked as an opening act for Pat Boone, Nipsy Russell, Redd Foxx and Bobby Darin, touring the United States, Italy, France, Holland, Germany, England and Canada. He was on the road with Dick Clark's Caravan of Stars, performed at Radio City Music Hall and did shows at the Fox Theatre with the legendary Alan Freed, the deejay who was famous for originally coining the expression "Rock & Roll." Bobby found that his great wit and emcee ability made him a special performer.

Bobby makes his home these days in Newark, New Jersey. He keeps a very active touring schedule and travels all over the country. We saw him at the Greek Theatre in Los Angeles in 1990, and he was dynamic!

I Was Tossin' And Turnin' All Night Thinkin' About Stuffed Calves Hearts

1 or more calves hearts (if whole, slice in half and scoop or cut out a well)
Garlic
Cayenne pepper
1/2 tsp ground nutmeg
1/2 tsp cloves
1/2 tsp brown sugar
Mushrooms
Salt
Herb bread stuffing
Walnuts
Heart pieces, chopped

In each half, season hearts as you like with garlic or garlic powder, cayenne pepper, nutmeg, cloves and salt. Mix mushrooms, walnuts, chopped heart pieces and bread stuffing and add to open heart. Pin together halves with wooden toothpicks, or skewer hearts after filling them. Season outside of hearts with remaining seasoning and wrap in heavy foil or a double wrap of regular foil. Fold foil to assure that no steam escapes. Place in baking pan. Bake at 350° for 1 1/2 hours or until you smell the flavor strongly. Enjoy!

Little Richard

Born and raised in Macon, Georgia, the third of fourteen children, Richard Wayne Penniman ("Little Richard") began singing in his local church choir while still a youngster. He signed with RCA Records in 1951 after winning a talent contest and released two singles, neither receiving prominent notice.

Returning to his job washing dishes in a Greyhound bus station, Richard sent a demo to Specialty Records, a fledgling Los Angeles label. The song, "Tutti Frutti," was his ticket out of the bus station to success and the beginning of an uninterrupted run of smash hits: "Long Tall Sally," "Rip It Up," "Lucille," "Jenny, Jenny," "Keep A Knockin'," "Good Golly, Miss Molly," "Ooh! My Soul" and "The Girl Can't Help It." By 1968, Little Richard had sold over 32 million records internationally.

A spiritual seeker whose religious revelations often conflicted with his Rock & Roll destiny, Richard ended his self-imposed industry hiatus in the mid-'80s. Back in the public spotlight, he received rave reviews for his appearance in the hit film *Down And Out In Beverly Hills*. In 1987, he was inducted into the Rock & Roll Hall Of Fame, and a year later he was spotlighted as a performer on the *60th Annual Academy Awards*. He has served as a TV commercial spokesperson for McDonald's and Taco Bell, and was recently paired with supermodel Cindy Crawford for Revlon's "Charlie" perfume.

Richard was honored with a star on the Hollywood Walk of Fame on June 21, 1990, and soon after, he returned to his hometown of Macon for the unveiling of Little Richard Penniman Boulevard. Most recently, he received the Lifetime Achievement Award from the National Academy of Recording Arts and Sciences. "Music is a way to spread joy," says Richard. "I've come to terms with that and with myself. You've got to do that before you can begin to help others."

Good Golly, It's Southern Homemade Brunswick Stew

2 Tbsp oil
1 beef chuck (3–4 lb)
1 1/2 tsp black pepper
4 medium onions, quartered
4 celery stalks, cut into pieces
4 bay leaves
3 beef-flavor bouillon cubes
(or 3 tsp beef-flavor instant bouillon)
2 tsp garlic powder
3 cups boiling water

2 cans (14 oz) peeled,
  diced tomatoes, in juice
1 can (14 oz) tomato sauce
6 medium potatoes, halved
6 medium carrots, cut into chunks
1 bag (10 oz) green peas
3 Tbsp flour
Lawry's seasoned salt (to taste)
3 Tbsp Worcestershire sauce

Heat oil over medium-high heat in a 5-qt pot. Brown meat, onion, celery, garlic and pepper for about 10 minutes. Add peeled tomatoes, tomato sauce, water, Worcestershire sauce, seasoned salt, beef-flavor and bay leaves. Cook on medium heat for 45 minutes. Add potatoes and carrots and cook for 15 minutes. Add 1/4 cup of cold water and flour, stirring to achieve thickness. Turn down heat. Add green peas. Let it simmer for about 30 minutes. Then it's ready. Now you have a pot of southern homemade Brunswick stew. Good to the last drop!

Peter and Gordon
Peter Asher

Peter Asher of Peter and Gordon is probably one of the few singers from the '60s to change careers (while still remaining in the music business) and become even more successful in his new field. After having such hits (singing with Gordon Waller) as "Lady Godiva" and "World Without Love," he has gone on to become one of the music industry's most renowned record producers. He has been awarded 29 gold albums and 18 platinum albums and, in both 1978 and 1989, was awarded the Grammy for Producer Of The Year.

From 1968 to 1970, Peter was head of A & R for Apple Records, The Beatles' newly formed record company. In this capacity he began producing James Taylor, whom he had signed to the label. Shortly after, he left Apple Records, moved to America and founded Peter Asher Management. In 1973, he also undertook the management and production of Linda Ronstadt, and the company began to expand. Today, Peter Asher Management represents Carole King, Little Feat, Joni Mitchell, Randy Newman and many other greats.

During his long and successful career, Peter has produced major hit recordings with such stars as Linda Ronstadt, 10,000 Maniacs, Cher, Diana Ross, Neil Diamond, Ringo Starr, Olivia Newton-John and countless other musical legends. Besides winning the two Producer Of The Year Grammys, he has also produced seven Grammy Award-winning records for other artists.

Lady Godiva's Spaghetti Carbonara

7 eggs
2 cups freshly grated Parmesan
   cheese
1/4 cup heavy or whipping cream
8 slices bacon

4 slices prosciutto
1 lb spaghetti
Olive oil
Butter
Black pepper

Cut the major chunks of fat off the bacon and separate the slices. Cut each slice into small segments. Add prosciutto, similarly sliced. In a bowl beat together eggs, Parmesan cheese, cream and a lot of black pepper. Start boiling the water for the spaghetti. Sauté the bacon and prosciutto in a lot of good olive oil, in as large a frying pan as you can find. When you guess that the mixture is about 10 minutes from being crisp and golden, put spaghetti into boiling water. After about 7 minutes, start to check every 30 seconds for the correct texture. When it seems right, drain spaghetti into a colander and put a chunk of butter into the pot. Return spaghetti to pot while it is still very hot. Pour the bacon/prosciutto/oil/fat mixture over it, followed rapidly by the eggy mixture. Stir, toss and mix it all up with a sense of urgency, since this is what is cooking the eggs. Put extra Parmesan on top and eat it!

The Rays
Harold "Hal" Miller

Hal Miller began his singing career at the age of thirteen, when he joined his church choir. His love of music led him to join the glee club in high school and a choral society in college. While in the service, Hal was a member of a barber shop quartet that toured and performed at different military base competitions.

After his discharge from the service, he became a "trouble shooter" at Emerson Radio and Television Plant where he met Harry James. Harry encouraged Hal to form a group with him. Walt Ford and David Jones were asked to join them, and The Rays were formed.

In 1956, the group met songwriters Bob Crewe and Frank Slay who had written a song called "Tippity Top." The Rays recorded it, and it became a minor hit on the East Coast, getting a lot of airplay from disc jockey Alan Freed. Then Crewe and Slay wrote another song called "Silhouettes." The Rays didn't like the song at all, but agreed to record it just the same—and the rest is history. It was an enormous hit that is still heard around the world today.

Hal is now retired and lives in Brooklyn, New York. He loves music as much as ever, and is an active member of The National Music Foundation.

Hal's Neckbones Supreme
(For Nice Silhouettes)

3 lbs fresh pork neck bones
1 cup celery, diced
1 cup onions, diced
1 can (15 oz) stewed tomatoes
1 can (16 oz) black-eyed peas
1 capful vinegar

2 cups water
Garlic powder
Seasoned salt (or salt and pepper)
Thyme
Worcestershire sauce
Gravy Master (optional)

Wash and clean neck bones. Season with garlic powder and seasoned salt or salt and pepper. Brown neck bones. Add celery, onions and sauté. Add stewed tomatoes, black-eyed peas, vinegar and water. Season with thyme and Worcestershire sauce. Cook until tender. Thicken gravy. Add Gravy Master if desired. Serve with rice and corn bread.

The Sex Pistols
Steve Jones

After The Sex Pistols' first and only album, *Never Mind The Bollocks, Here's The Sex Pistols*, Rock & Roll music was never the same. *Rolling Stone* ranked the album number two on its list of the Top 100—second only to The Beatles' *Sgt. Pepper*. The singles, "Anarchy In The UK" and "God Save The Queen," signaled the dawn of the punk revolution. "God Save The Queen" soared to number one on the British charts despite being banned from radio airplay.

Besides changing music forever, the Pistols also altered fashion and attitudes by reflecting the confusion, insecurity and anger teenagers were feeling worldwide. Rock critic Robert Hilburn has written that, "However calculated the Pistol's anarchy image was, the Pistols delivered musically. *Bollocks* stands as one of the truly incandescent moments in rock."

On the album it was Steve Jones who delivered the music, co-writing the songs and playing all the guitar and bass, since Sid Vicious was in no condition to perform. But as Steve became more serious about their music, Vicious and Johnny "Rotten" Lydon were growing less so and the band came apart during its 1978 U.S. tour.

Since that cataclysmic bust-up, Steve has moved to Los Angeles and worked consistently with various musicians: Blondie, Joan Jett, Duran Duran's Andy Taylor and Iggy Pop, as well as recording two

solo albums: *Mercy* and *Fire and Gasoline*.

Steve says, "The Pistols weren't just another band. We made a mark on Rock & Roll history, and there's respect in that. We were for a time period, like The Beatles were for their time, and it will always be with me. But I want people to like me for my music, not for any hype. Today I feel I'm a good musician and can write as good as anyone. I have my own sound. Now I can say I'm a musican and believe in it."

Pie And Mash

1/2 lb of some weird old minced meat
Mashed potatoes
Pie shell

Put meat into a pie shell with 2
dollops of mashed potatoes on top.
Bake for 30 minutes at 400°. Best
eaten with your fingers.

Dee Dee Sharp

Philadelphia-born Dee Dee Sharp learned to sing and play the piano in her grandfather's church. In 1961, her mother was in a serious car accident, and Dee Dee wanted to help out with the household bills. "So I answered a newspaper ad for session singers. Because I could read music and play keyboards, I was hired." She was only fourteen years old when she found herself singing back-up on recording sessions for such greats as Frankie Avalon, Freddie Cannon and Chubby Checker.

Then, one short year later, she recorded her first single, "Mashed Potato Time." It soared to number one, and she had the whole world doing the Mashed Potatoes. It was followed by "Gravy For My Mashed Potatoes," "Ride," "Do The Bird," "Rock Me In The Cradle Of Love," "Wild," "Where Did I Go Wrong" and "I Really Love You." All were solid Top 20 hits. That same year she also teamed up with Chubby Checker and recorded the smash hit "Slow Twistin'." Her music has recently been heard in such films as *Sister Act*, *Hairspray*, *Desperately Seeking Susan* and *Troop Beverly Hills*.

Today, Dee Dee still makes her home on the East Coast and continues to perform. Among her many distinctions, she holds a doctorate in Psychology from the University of Pennsylvania, has been honored with a Life Achievement Award by the Philadelphia Music Foundation, has raised thousands of dollars for the United Negro College Fund, and was recently signed by Maybelline, the cosmetics firm, to write and record radio commercials for its new "Shades of You" products. In the summer of 1990, we reunited with Dee Dee at a concert in Sarasota, Florida, to benefit The National Music Foundation. It was the first time we had seen her in many years and we were very happy to renew our friendship. Since that time, we speak often on the phone and continue to keep in touch.

Mashed Potato Shepherd's Pie

1 1/2–2 lbs ground sirloin
6–8 potatoes, diced
1/4 stick margarine or butter
1/2 cup celery, chopped
1 onion, chopped
1/2 cup green peppers, diced
1/4 tsp dry mustard

1/4 tsp onion powder
1/4 tsp seasoned salt
1/4 tsp garlic powder
1/2 cup evaporated milk
1/3 cup Wesson Extra Light
   Vegetable Oil (or olive oil)

Place oil in saucepan over low flame. Add ground sirloin. Stir in celery, peppers and onions. Do not overcook. Add garlic powder, dry mustard, onion powder, seasoned salt and continue to stir until onions and meat are tender but not brown. Place in 3-qt casserole dish.

Wash, peel and dice potatoes. Place in 4-qt saucepan and cover with water (do not add salt). Cook until tender. Drain and whip with 1/4 stick of margarine or butter and 1/2 cup evaporated milk. Beat until stiff. Add to the top of casserole containing meat.

Bake at 350° for 50–60 minutes. Edges should be lightly brown; top should be brown. Serve hot with gravy (recipe follows). Can be prepared and frozen for later. Serve with greens.

Gravy for Mashed Potato Shepherd's Pie

2 tsp flour
1/3 cup Wesson Extra Light Vegetable Oil
1/2 cup stock (use beef or chicken stock)
1 cup warm water
1/4 cup onions

Place oil in 10" frying pan over low flame. Add flour, stirring constantly with wooden spoon until brown. Add stock. Continue stirring until mixture has dissolved. Add onion and water. Season to taste with salt and pepper. Stir, then cover and let simmer until onions are tender. Serve over pie.

Connie Stevens

In 1959 and 1960, Connie Stevens was America's sweetheart on the charts. Her sexy, identifiable voice was first heard on the hit record "Kookie, Kookie, Lend Me Your Comb," with Ed "Kookie" Byrnes. At the time, Ed played the adored "Kookie" on one of the most popular TV shows of the day, *77 Sunset Strip*. The record was produced by the talented Donald Ralke, who later produced such major hits as "The Birds And The Bees," "The Mountain's High" and "One Boy." Ralke was doing the music for the TV show at the time and went on to produce Connie's next big hit, "Sixteen Reasons," one of the biggest romantic hits of 1960.

Connie's endearing and classic role as "Cricket" in the long-running ABC TV series *Hawaiian Eye* brought her to the public eye. Subsequently, she went on to star in the TV series *Wendy and Me* with the legendary George Burns. Familiar to both movie and TV audiences, Connie maintains a steady line of roles in current films and TV shows while making regular appearances on the concert stage.

Her daughters, Joely and Tricia Fisher, join their mom in concert as back-up singers. In 1990, Connie performed a sell-out concert tour that took her from Florida and the Southeast to Nevada and the San Francisco Bay Area. She continues her usual engagements in Las Vegas, Atlantic City and Lake Tahoe, as well as other major venues throughout the country and abroad. With a whirlwind schedule of touring, film and TV commitments and developing theatrical projects for her own Shane Productions, she tirelessly devotes herself to charity work. A major portion of her time and support goes to Project Windfeather, an organization she founded to help the plight of Native Americans—she's part Iroquois.

Sixteen Reasons Why You'll Love My Italian Meat Sauce

1 1/4 lb hamburger meat
1 medium onion, finely chopped
3 cloves garlic, finely chopped
1 large can tomato puree
   (make sure it's puree)
1 can (18 oz) tomato sauce

1 can (6 oz) tomato paste
1 tsp (or more) sweet basil
2 bay leaves
1 tsp sugar, level
Olive oil
Salt and pepper

Brown onion, garlic and sweet basil in a little olive oil. Add salt and pepper. After onion is yellowish, add hamburger meat and brown. Then add tomato puree, sauce and paste and equal amounts of water from each can. Add sugar and bay leaves. Cover and simmer for 1 hour. Take cover off and simmer another hour. You can brown mushrooms when browning the onions but that's optional. Serves 6.

Brenton Wood

Boogum" (hence his "Oogum Boogum Lite Chile") and "Baby You Got It."

Over the years, Brenton's music has taken him to Germany, France, Belgium, Mexico and Italy, where he played the San Remo Festival with Stevie Wonder. Today, he resides in Los Angeles and has just completed a new album for Beck Wood Records called *That's The Deal*, a mixture of jazz, soul, R & B and rap which also features "Oogum Boogum."

Brenton was one of the first of our old friends who became actively involved in The National Music Foundation. He, along with Tommy Roe, Brian Hyland, The Safaris, Rosie And The Originals, Dodie Stevens, Chuck "The Champs" Rio, Little Caesar And The Romans and Pete Rivera of Rare Earth joined us in putting on one of the first fund-raising shows on the West Coast. Brenton was great and performed all of his hits, which, by the way, were written by him.

When he's not recording, writing or performing, Brenton concentrates on his other interests which include old cars and spending time with his family and golden retriever. He is deeply committed to helping promote the importance of education and being drug-free.

In 1967, Alfred Smith took a bus from Compton, California, to Hollywood and quickly changed his name to Brenton Wood. He actually recorded his first record, "Too Fat," however, in 1959, when he was still a teenager and known as Little Freddie. But his real record success followed after he became Brenton Wood, and in the '60s and '70s he had such Top Ten hits as "Gimme A Little Sign," "Oogum

Oogum Boogum Lite Chile

1/2 lb ground beef
2 cups pinto beans, cooked
1/2 brown onion
1 tsp seasoning salt

1/2 tsp garlic salt
1/2 tsp black pepper
1 can tomato sauce
1 pkg Texas Chili Mix (to taste)

Break ground beef in small chunks and cook over low flame. Pour beef fat off. Knead ground beef with fork. Pour tomato sauce into pan and mix with seasonings and onion. Then pour into pot of beans. Simmer to delite.

Frank Zappa

Frank Zappa defies any category or label. As leader of The Mothers of Invention—one of the weirdest and most brilliant experimental bands ever—and perennial iconoclast, Zappa has earned a prime spot in Rock & Roll lore!

In Lancaster, California, Zappa formed his first garage band, The Black Outs, and later joined The Soul Giants, which became The Mothers of Invention. The Mothers were known for their innovative music and satirical, insightful lyrics. While all of his colleagues were turning on and tuning in, Zappa never did drugs. In fact, "Flower Punk" on *We're Only In It For The Money*, lampoons the '60s culture, hippies and love-ins.

Frank has always fought censorship and even distributed a poster of himself stark naked on a toilet and called it "Phi Krappa Zappa." It makes sense that the first chapter of his autobiography is titled "How Weird Am I Anyway?"

Zappa has released more than 50 albums, including his ground-breaking, brain-breaking debut *Freak Out* as well as *200 Motels* (also the name of his cult classic film starring Ringo Starr), *Sheik Yerobuti* and *Jazz From Hell*. Funnily enough, Frank's biggest-selling single "Valley Girl" featured his daughter Moon Unit Zappa gagging people with a spoon all over America.

Even within a single song, Zappa's music has ranged from garage rock to pop, jazz to classical. He is a respected composer in Europe, having had his music recorded by the London Symphony Orchestra, among others.

His acute sociopolitical observations (he rails at America's "cryptofascist" education and economic systems) and plain irreverence have impressed and infuriated many. Zappa remains a prominent advocate of free speech—having testified before the Senate Commerce Committee against censorship. He has relished going after fashion, hypocrisy and stereotypes, managing to offend an amazing array of people and at the same time garner stacks of die-hard fans.

Burnt Weenie Sandwich

1 Hebrew National weenie
2 pieces of bread
Mustard
   Take weenie, put it on a fork and
burn it on the stove. Wrap bread around
burnt weenie. Squirt some mustard on it
and bite.

The Collector's Page

RICHIE VALENS

For information on how to order this Rock 'n' Roll/ Rhythm and Blues Commemorative Stamp, please see page 2.

7
Breads and Desserts

My Boyfriend's Back 'Cause He Loves My Mocha Cheesecake
J.T. 's Cornbread
Stayin' Alive On Macaroon And Vanilla Custard Dessert
Hold Me, Thrill Me, Taste by Cornbread
Tequila Sweetie Pies
What'd I Say? I Said I Want Pineapple Upside Down Cake
Charlie Brown's Peanut Cookie Delight
Bo Diddley's A Custard Pie Slinger
40 Miles Of Banana Bread
Michael's Maple Pecan Butter Cookies
Gary's Magic Diamond Bars
I Will Follow Him Into The Kitchen And Make Crispy Cherry Bake
Papa-Oom-Mow-Mow Candi Carrot Pie
Kisses Sweeter Than Wine Cake
Corn Muffins Ronstadt
Angel Baby's Angel Food Cake
Image Of A Swirl (A Marble Cake)
Pineapple Crush Pie
I Met Him On A Sundae
Mama Said Bake Cranberry Bread
Since I Don't Have Shoo-fly Pie
Auntie Carol's You Can Hardly Bear It Carat Cake
Do I Do Oatmeal Cookies

The Angels

The Angels, Phyllis "Jiggs" Sirico and Peggy Santiglia Davison, have been recording and performing together since they were teenagers in Orange and Belleville, New Jersey, and, according to this popular classic duo, they have been best friends all that time. Between 1961 and 1964, The Angels recorded six chart records including the classic, "My Boyfriend's Back."

When "My Boyfriend's Back" was released, it seemed to be an instant hit. Peggy was on vacation when Jiggs called her. "Come back home now! Our record

is a giant hit!" The Angels received nationwide attention for the sensational million-seller that was definitely one of the more graphic teenage statements of that time. The record took the industry by storm and set a style, pace and sound still emulated by female groups today.

As The Angels, Jiggs and Peggy traveled the world and appeared on all the major TV shows of the day: *American Bandstand*, *Ed Sullivan*, *The Tonight Show Starring Johnny Carson*, *The Dean Martin Show*, *Midnight Special* and many others. They also toured throughout the United States, Canada, Europe and South America.

Jiggs has acted, modeled and/or sung in numerous commercials including spots for Caravelle Watches, Thom McAnn Shoes and Russ Togs clothing line. Her many voice-overs included one for Multimedia Education Productions for Research for Better Schools.

Peggy has been a staff songwriter for April Blackwood Music in New York where she wrote the song "Beggin' " with Bob Gaudio for Frankie Valli. She also toured and recorded with The Serendipity Singers in the late '60s.

Although both women have individually pursued separate endeavors over the years, they can be found today performing as The Angels once again. A recent successful Grammy appearance and a made-for-TV movie entitled *My Boyfriend's Back* continue to keep them in the forefront of classic early rockers.

My Boyfriend's Back 'Cause He Loves My Mocha Cheesecake

BASIC CRUMMY CRUST

1 1/2 cups vanilla wafer crumbs
6 Tbsp butter
1/4 cup granulated sugar

Preheat oven to 350°. Place crumbs in bowl and add butter and sugar, mixing well. Press crumb mixture onto bottom and partly up sides of greased 8" spring-form pan and smooth mixture along bottom evenly. Bake for 10 minutes, cool before filling.

CHEESECAKE

6 squares (6 oz) semi-sweet chocolate
1 1/2 lbs cream cheese
1/2 cup granulated sugar
2 large eggs
1 cup heavy cream
1/3 cup double-strength coffee (easiest way
   to make double strength is to use instant
   coffee—experiment with new flavored
   coffees or even with instant espresso)
1 tsp vanilla extract

Melt chocolate in top of double boiler. In large mixing bowl, beat cream cheese and sugar until light. Add eggs, 1 at a time, beating thoroughly after each. Beat in cream. Pour melted chocolate slowly into cheese mixture and add coffee and vanilla, mixing to blend ingredients thoroughly. Pour mixture into prepared crust and bake 45 minutes or until edges are puffed up slightly. Cool in oven, with door cracked open. Remove and cool to room temperature. Refrigerate and eat.

The B-52's
Fred Schneider

Fifteen years into a career that began as a low-rent, new-wave lark in Athens, Georgia, The B-52's have become an integral part of our homegrown musical cosmos. From "Rock Lobster" and "Private Idaho" to "Channel Z" and "Love Shack," The B-52's have wrapped their goofy, colorful sense of the absurd around infectious dance-rock tunes, starting a party every time the music begins.

"Love Shack," written about a "liberal" nightclub in Atlanta, hit number three, from the album *Cosmic Thing* which reached number four on the U.S. charts. *Rolling Stone* voted "Love Shack" the Best Single of 1989.

"We're out there to entertain people," says lead singer Fred Schneider, "but it's great to get people thinking and dancing at the same time." Lyrics on the B-52's latest album, *Good Stuff*, urge listeners to respect both the environment and their own individualism, regardless of society's conformist pressures. "We've turned up the volume on our rage," says Keith Strickland, "and we're saying things that we feel we need to say."

The B-52's have always supported various progressive causes, donating their efforts to numerous benefits. "We focus on AIDS organizations (the group lost member Ricky Wilson to AIDS in 1985), environmental concerns and animal rights," Kate Pierson explains. "Music changes people and people can change the world."

"Years ago I wanted a classic (and the best) cornbread recipe," explains Fred. "My friend, John Taylor, now an author and owner of Hoppin' John's Cookbook Store in Charleston, says this simple, delicious cornbread is a traditional recipe from the Old South. Jazz it up to your taste though."

J.T.'s Cornbread

1 3/4 cups cornmeal
2 cups buttermilk (or yogurt)
1 egg
1 tsp baking soda
1 tsp baking powder
1/2 tsp salt
Optional: chilies, chopped onions,
  shredded cheddar

   Preheat oven to 450° and preheat 8" skillet or pan. Mix buttermilk, egg, baking soda, baking powder and salt. Add cornmeal and any optional ingredients and bake 15–20 minutes until top is golden brown and tester comes out clean.

The Bee Gees
Barry Gibb

Five-time Grammy Award winners, The Bee Gees are indisputably one of the most popular recording acts of all time. Their records have sold more than 100 million copies around the world, and their soundtrack album for 1977's *Saturday Night Fever* sold a remarkable 30 million copies, making it the best-selling album of all time until Michael Jackson took away the title with his *Thriller* album. The double album set featured three number-one American singles: "How Deep Is Your Love," "Stayin' Alive" and "Night Fever."

The Bee Gees (the Brothers Gibb) are the sons of bandleader and drummer Hugh and singer Barbara, born on the Isle of Man in the Irish Sea. The three brothers first performed together in 1955 as The Rattlesnakes, when Barry was nine and the twin brothers, Robin and Maurice, were only seven. In 1958, the Gibb family moved to Australia where they released many singles and one album on the Festival label. By the time their eleventh single made it to the top of the charts "down under" in 1967, the family was on a five-week boat trip to England in search of greener pastures. Within weeks of arriving in London, The Bee Gees signed with Robert Stigwood and NEMS—the same management company that worked with The Beatles.

Today, Barry Gibb and his wife, Linda (a former Miss Edinburgh), reside in Miami Beach and also have a home in England. They have been married for 22 years and have five children.

Stayin' Alive On Macaroon And Vanilla Custard Dessert

1 dozen macaroons
1 pkg Bird's custard mix
2 cups milk
4 Tbsp sugar

1/2 cup sherry
3 egg whites
1 tsp lemon juice

Crumble macaroons into bottom of a baking dish; moisten with sherry and cover with custard (which has been prepared according to package instructions). Make meringue by whipping egg whites until soft, then slowly add 1 Tbsp sugar and beat until stiff. Beat in lemon juice and spread generously over pudding. Bake in the oven at 325° until brown. Serve warm.

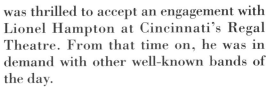

Mel Carter

Mel Carter cut his first "record" when he was only four years old. His grandmother held the microphone while he sang a Negro spiritual in one of those twenty-five-cent recording booths that were found in penny arcades. His talent encouraged his family to help launch his career. At the age of nine, following years of experience entertaining at church functions and on local radio shows, Mel was thrilled to accept an engagement with Lionel Hampton at Cincinnati's Regal Theatre. From that time on, he was in demand with other well-known bands of the day.

In 1960, Mel made the trek from Ohio to Los Angeles when the "fortune" on a penny-arcade scale popped out the advice: "Go west young man." Once in Los Angeles, he appeared at such spots as Ciro's with Dinah Washington and The Crescendo with Bessie Griffin's Gospel Pearls and in Las Vegas with Damita Jo.

When his first major recording contract came, Mel had already had some experience as a recording artist on Sam Cooke's label. His rendition of "When A Boy Falls In Love" had been high on the charts in England as well as in the United States. His biggest single to date, "Hold Me, Thrill Me, Kiss Me," became a Top 10 hit in America and within a year Mel enjoyed a smash engagement at the world-famous Coconut Grove.

In 1985, Mel's album *Willing* won him a Grammy nomination for Best Performance.

Mel continues to perform (we watched him from the wings as he recently "brought the house down" at the Greek Theatre in Los Angeles). He has been seen in many commercials, movies and TV shows. In his spare time, Mel works with youth groups in Los Angeles teaching music and harmonies and is an amateur horticulturist.

Hold Me, Thrill Me, Taste My Cornbread

1 1/2 cups yellow cornmeal
1/2 cup flour
4 tsp baking powder
1/2 tsp salt
1/4 cup sugar

1 cup milk
1 egg, beaten
1/2 cup corn oil
1 can (16 oz) crea- style corn

Mix dry ingredients in bowl. Mix milk, egg and corn oil together and add to dry ingredients. Stir to mix, then add corn. Fill greased baking pan 1/2 full. Bake at 425° for 25 minutes or until lightly browned. Serve with butter.

The Champs
Chuck Rio

In 1957, Chuck Rio of The Champs wrote what was to become a classic—"Tequila." He also played saxophone on the recording, and it is Chuck's low voice that says the word "Tequila." Released in 1958 on Challenge Records, the record took the world by storm. The very next year, Chuck Rio and The Champs were presented with the first R & B Grammy Award ever given, and as the composer, Chuck received the BMI Achievement Award for the most popular song of the year. Since its release, "Tequila" has been used in such movies as *Pepe, Cheech & Chong's Next Movie, Losing It, Big Wednesday, Pee Wee's Big Adventure* and *Peggy Sue Got Married.* It has also been heard in TV shows such as *Moon-lighting* and *Miami Vice.*

Over the years, The Champs have had a total of seven chart records including "Too Much Tequila" and "Limbo Rock." They appeared on *The Ed Sullivan Show* and Dick Clark's *American Bandstand.*

Today Chuck and his talented wife, Sharee, live in Midway, California, and have never stopped making music. Sharee has had several of her own hits in the Latin field including the Spanish version of "You Light Up My Life," which went to number two on the Latin charts. She is now the female singer with The Champs Band as they continue to perform in Las Vegas, Reno, Lake Tahoe and The Forum in Los Angeles. They were also wonderful when they did a benefit show with us for The National Music Foundation.

Tequila Sweetie Pies

1 cup sugar
1/2 cup butter
2 eggs, beaten
1 tsp vanilla
1/2 cup chopped dates

1/2 cup English walnuts
1 Tbsp coconut
3 drops Tequila
1 pkg pie crust mix, prepared
    according to instructions

Cream together sugar and butter, then mix with remaining ingredients. Line cupcake pans with pie crust. Fill with mixture and bake for 30 minutes at 350° or until golden brown. Enjoy!

Ray Charles

Ray Charles Robinson was not born blind, only poor. "You hear folks talking about being poor," he recounts. "Even compared to other blacks...we were on the bottom of the ladder looking up at everyone else. Nothing below us except the ground." It took three years, starting when Ray Charles was only four, for the country boy who loved to look at the blazing sun at its height, the boy who loved to try to catch lightning, the boy who loved to strike matches to see their fierce, brief glare, to travel the path from light to darkness. But Ray has almost seven years of sight memory—colors, the images of backwoods country and the face of the most important person in his early life: his mother, Aretha Robinson.

Ray Charles was accepted as a charity student at St. Augustine's, the Florida state school for the deaf and blind. He learned Braille and how to type. He became a skilled basket weaver and was allowed to develop his great gift of music. He discovered mathematics and its correlation to music. He learned to compose and arrange music in his head, singing out the parts one by

one. Ray remained at St. Augustine's until his mother's death, after which he set out on the road for the first time as a struggling professional musician.

Seattle, Washington, was a turning point for Ray. He became a minor celebrity in local clubs where he met another younger musician, Quincy Jones, marking the beginning of an intertwining of the lives of two musical giants.

Ray has had more hits than we could mention. Among the most famous are "What'd I Say," "Georgia On My Mind," "Hit The Road Jack," "Unchain My Heart," "Born To Lose," "Busted" and countless others.

What'd I Say? I Said I Want Pineapple Upside Down Cake

2 sticks butter (1 cup)
2 cups sugar
3 1/2 cups all-purpose flour, sifted
3 1/2 tsp baking powder
4 eggs
1/2 tsp vanilla
1 1/4 cups whole milk
Brown sugar
Maraschino cherries
1 can pineapple rings

Cream 1 stick butter and sugar and add eggs. Mix in dry ingredients gradually with milk, adding vanilla last. Melt 1 stick butter in 14" x 11" pan. Add light brown sugar to cover surface of pan. Place sliced pineapple over brown sugar, then place a maraschino cherry in each hole of pineapple. Cover with batter and bake approximately 30–45 minutes at 350° or until straw or toothpick inserted in cake is dry when removed. When cake is done, remove from oven and turn upside down on flat surface. Should be delicious!

The Coasters
Carl Gardner

Carl Gardner, the original lead singer of The Coasters, was born in Tyler, Texas, in 1928. In 1955, he and three other young men formed The Coasters—but this was not Carl's first "group" experience. In the early '50s, as lead singer for The Robins, Carl had his first hit with a Leiber and Stoller song called "Smokey Joe's Cafe." It was primarily a "West Coast hit," but quickly got the attention of Atlantic Records. Due to some group friction, Carl and one other member of The Robins left to form The Coasters, and the rest is history.

One of the most popular early Rock & Roll groups, The Coasters had an amazing string of hits from 1956 to 1964, including "Down In Mexico," "Young Blood," "Searchin'," "Yakety Yak," "Charlie Brown," "Along Came Jones," "Poison Ivy," "Little Egypt" and "Love Potion No. 9." Their hits were written by Leiber and Stoller, two of the most successful songwriters of the day.

Today, Carl Gardner resides in Port St. Lucie, Florida, with his lovely wife, Veta, who also happens to be The Coasters' manager. Carl continues to perform his incredible hits to enthusiastic crowds of old and new fans alike. Those wonderful hits of the '50s and '60s will live on forever.

Charlie Brown's Peanut Cookie Delight

1/2 cup (1 stick) butter or margarine
1 cup sugar
1 egg
3/4 cup flour
1/2 tsp baking powder

1/2 tsp baking soda
1 cup rolled oats
1/2 cup salted peanuts, chopped
1 cup cornflakes

Cream butter and sugar together. Add egg and beat well. Sift flour, baking soda and baking powder together, and fold into creamed mixture. Add rolled oats, peanuts and cornflakes, and mix well.

Drop by teaspoonfuls onto greased baking sheet leaving room for them to spread. Bake 10 minutes. Makes about 40 cookies. These cookies are very crisp and keep well.

Bo Diddley

Bo Diddley was born Ellas McDaniel in Mississippi's cotton country. Raised by relatives, he moved with them to Chicago at age seven. There he got the nickname Bo Diddley, (meaning a mischievous or "bully" boy), which he used as an amateur and semi-pro boxer.

Bo's musical instruction began with formal training on violin and trombone, but after receiving a guitar for Christmas when he was ten, he taught himself open-tuned guitar. In his early teens, he formed a combo and began playing street corners. After leaving school at sixteen, he did some boxing and then formed a band to work the blues clubs on Chicago's South Side.

In 1955, he auditioned for Chess Records with a song he wrote called "Uncle John." Chess Records liked it and signed Bo. They felt, however, that the song needed some rewriting and a title change—so Bo named it after himself, did a rewrite, and recorded it in 35 minutes. The reworked song, "Bo Diddley," became one of the year's biggest hits.

While on a break at a recording session in 1959, Bo came up with another classic hit. He and maracas player, Jerome Green, were kidding around when Ron Maylow of Chess Records turned on the tape recorder in the control room. About ten minutes later Ron turned it off and told Bo, who was surprised and couldn't figure out why he'd done that. After much editing, the song was released, and "Say Man" was a smash.

Bo enjoyed a wide following and it seemed everyone liked him. In the mid-'50s, whenever Bo played the Apollo Theatre in Harlem, a young Elvis Presley would come to watch him work. In 1962, Bo performed a private show at the White House at the request of President Kennedy.

The '70s actually found Bo as the sheriff in Los Lunas, New Mexico. But he missed his music and had to get back to it. Consequently, 1992 was one of his busiest years, performing five to seven days a week all over the world.

Bo Diddley's A Custard Pie Slinger

1 dozen eggs
2 cups sugar
1 stick butter
2 heaping tsp flour

2 tsp baking powder
1 tsp nutmeg (or to taste)
1 1/2 cups milk
3 deep-dish pie crusts, pre-baked

Melt butter. Gradually blend in sugar. Add rest of ingredients and mix in blender. Fill 3 deep dish pie pans already lined with favorite crust (graham cracker or regular pie crust). Bake in oven at 375° until brown. Let cool and enjoy.

Duane Eddy

Few artists have had a greater impact on guitars and guitar players than Duane Eddy. He's the only solo instrumentalist to have achieved Top 10 placings in the U.S. and U.K. charts in every decade from the '50s through the '80s, and since his first recording in 1957, "Movin' 'n' Groovin'," he has sold over 100 million records.

Duane was born in Corning, New York, on April 26, 1938. By the age of sixteen, after moving with his family to Phoenix, Arizona, he was playing his guitar regularly in local clubs and appearing on TV and radio programs. After studying recording studio techniques at Audio Recorders in Phoenix, Duane realized that the bass strings of the guitar recorded more solidly than the high strings. From this discovery, the trademark Duane Eddy "Twangy Guitar" sound was born. His 1958 album, *Have Twangy Guitar, Will Travel*, was one of the first Rock & Roll albums to be recorded in stereo.

He toured throughout most of the '60s, before deciding to take time off to work as a producer with artists such as Waylon Jennings and Phil Everly. Fortunately for guitar fans, he resumed touring and recording, often joined by stars who grew up listening to his records, including Paul McCartney, George Harrison, Huey Lewis, Ry Cooder and Jeff Lynne.

Duane wanted to share some cooking tips: "Mom says to add the baking soda to the bananas and mash them together first, and since this is really her recipe, you'd better do it her way. Something about 'fluffier' bananas (whatever that means). I grew up on this bread and my grandchildren are eating it now. Hope you enjoy it as much as all the Eddys do."

40 Miles Of Banana Bread

3 extremely ripe bananas
  (they should look bad)
1 tsp baking soda
1 tsp salt
1 generous cup sugar
1/2 cup shortening
  (Mom used Crisco)
2 eggs
2 cups flour

Pre-heat oven to 350°. Mash bananas in large bowl. Add soda and salt. Beat in eggs, sugar and shortening. Add flour a bit at a time, beating until batter is smooth. Pour into greased loaf pan, (a Bundt pan will work as well). Bake at 350° for approximately 45 minutes, or until toothpick inserted into the center comes out clean.

Michael Jackson

He is—without question—the King of Pop. He is also the most talked-about entertainer in history. His artistic skills, whether in the recording studio or on a concert stage, are legendary. But there is more to the man than simply his electrifying performances.

Born in Gary, Indiana, on August 29, Michael, along with his brothers, auditioned for record mogul Berry Gordy when Michael was only eleven years old. The year was 1969, and Gordy's Detroit-based Motown Records signed the group immediately. The fledgling recording act scored an impressive four consecutive number-one singles over the next two years, and The Jackson Five transcended all barriers of race and age in their appeal.

Of course, for Michael, that was just the beginning. Since then he has continued with tremendous success. According to the Guinness Book of World Records, his *Thriller* album is the largest selling album in history. It also received a record of seven American Music Awards and eight Grammy Awards. On February 24, 1993, Michael was honored with the Grammy Living Legend Award—and that is truly what he is!

Michael Jackson has taken good fortune and parlayed it into a benevolent empire of philanthropic conscience, trumpeting the messages of humanity and peace around the world. His hands-on contributions and selfless attitude regarding tomorrow's generation continue to inspire young and old alike.

Michael's Maple Pecan Butter Cookies

1 cup unsalted butter
2/3 cup maple syrup
1/3 cup maple sugar
1 tsp vanilla
1 1/2 cups unbleached flour

1/2 cup whole-wheat flour
1/4 tsp baking soda
1/4 tsp sea salt
1 cup pecans, chopped

Pre-heat oven to 350°. In an electric mixer, cream butter with maple syrup, maple sugar and vanilla until very creamy and light. In a separate bowl combine flours with other dry ingredients. Mix lightly with butter mixture until flour is blended in and fold in pecans. Do not overmix. Drop by teaspoonfuls onto a cookie sheet covered with parchment paper (or lightly buttered). Bake 10 – 12 minutes. Watch out—they're *dangerous!*

Gary Lewis & The Playboys
Gary Lewis

Gary Lewis & The Playboys were discovered by producer Snuff Garrett during the summer of 1964. With Snuff and arranger Leon Russell behind them, their first single, "This Diamond Ring," went straight to number one. After their second hit, "Count Me In," went to number two, Gary and the band proved that they could be a continued success. More Top 10 hits followed such as "Save Your Heart For Me," "Everybody Loves A Clown," "She's Just My Style," "Sure Gonna Miss Her" and many more.

In 1965, Gary was *Cash Box* magazine's "Male Vocalist Of The Year," winning the honor over nominees Elvis Presley and Frank Sinatra. He was also the first and only artist during the '60s to have his first seven releases reach *Billboard* magazine's Top 10 on the Hot 100 Chart. In the Philippines during this time, Gary Lewis & The Playboys were considered "America's Answer to The Beatles," and over a two-week period they sold out the 18,000-capacity Arianeta Coliseum for 24 performances. Along with his appearances on such popular TV shows as *American Bandstand*, *The Joey Bishop Show* and *The Tonight Show Starring Johnny Carson*, Gary accumulated an impressive five appearances within two years on *The Ed Sullivan Show*.

After his last appearance on *The Ed Sullivan Show*, Gary was drafted, and on New Year's Day, 1967, he officially entered the Army for two years where he served in combat. He spent his leave in the studio and recorded "Sealed With A Kiss" and "Everybody Loves A Clown."

Gary and his wife, Patty, live in Ohio, and Gary continues to tour and entertain fans across the country and abroad.

Gary's Magic Diamond Bars

1/2 cup melted butter
1 1/2 cups graham
   cracker crumbs
1 cup nuts, chopped
3 1/2 oz coconut,
   shredded
1 bag chocolate chips
1 can Eagle Brand milk

   Mix melted butter with graham cracker crumbs. Pat into bottom of 9" x 13" pan. Layer nuts and chocolate chips and sprinkle shredded coconut over top. Pour milk over top and bake at 350° for 25 minutes. Let cool before cutting.

Little Peggy March

Peggy March was five years old when she won her first singing contest, which led to her becoming a regular on *Rex Trailor's Stars Of Tomorrow*, a popular TV show in the Philadelphia area. By the time she was thirteen, she was a seasoned pro.

Peggy was heard singing at a wedding by someone who decided to contact RCA Records. This led to an RCA recording contract, and her first recording, "I Will Follow Him," was an instant, monster smash hit. RCA heard about Peggy's way with language—she had a phenomenal ear and could pick up a language in a very short time—and decided to go after a worldwide market. With "I Will Follow Him" number one in the U.S., Peggy recorded the song in French, Spanish, Italian, Dutch, Japanese and German. She literally had the number-one record in the world! Since her professional poise was far beyond her years, it was hard to believe that Peggy would be unable to take advantage of the appearance offers coming in from all over the country. But strict laws prohibiting minors from performing in establishments that served alcohol stopped her. She had to go abroad to show what she was capable of doing in the world of entertainment and her performances in every country in Europe were tremendous successes.

Peggy is married, has a daughter, Sande, and has moved from California to Florida. Currently thinking of moving to Germany, she speaks fluent German and is always in demand there as an entertainer. She writes songs and has had success writing for Pia Zadora and Audrey Landers and has taken assignments to write English translations for songs in other languages.

LITTLE PEGGY MARCH

I Will Follow Him Into The Kitchen And Make Crispy Cherry Bake

2 cups dark sweet cherries, fresh or
  frozen, thawed and drained
2 Tbsp vegetable oil
3 1/2 Tbsp tapioca
1/2 cup unsweetened pineapple
  concentrate (frozen juice concentrate)
2 Tbsp water

1 tsp almond extract
Topping:
1/2 cup rolled oats
1/4 cup oat or whole-wheat flour
3 Tbsp vegetable oil
1/4 tsp cinnamon
1/4 cup almonds, chopped

Pre-heat oven to 350°. Oil 8" x 8" x 2" glass baking dish. In a large bowl, stir together all ingredients, except topping. Pour mixture into prepared baking dish and let sit for 10 minutes. In a small bowl stir together all topping ingredients with a fork. Sprinkle topping over cherry mixture and bake 50 minutes. Remove dish from oven and cool on a wire rack. Serve warm or cold, with whipped cream, ice cream or all by itself.

The Rivingtons
Al Frazier

In 1962, four young men from South Central Los Angeles decided to form a singing group. Little did they know that the song they came up with would become a Rock & Roll standard. By June of the same year, everyone was walking around singing "Papa-Oom-Mow-Mow."

Being a Rivington was not Al Frazier's first "group" experience. While still in high school, he formed his first vocal group called The Mello Moods, which included fellow classmate Paul Robi, who would later find fame as a member of The Platters.

When The Rivingtons first formed, producer/arranger Ernie Freeman thought they needed some work and decided to use them as background voices on various sessions. "We knew Ernie Freeman very well," says Al, "and we did a lot of stuff with him. He needed a group right away to do back-up for this little fifteen-year-old kid who he said was going to make stars out of us. The kid turned out to be Paul Anka and we sang on his first record, 'Blau-Wile-Deveest-Fontaine.' A group called The Jacks got credit for the background vocals, but it was really us."

After "Papa-Oom-Mow-Mow" was re-corded, they decided to take it over to Capitol Records and play it for them. When Capitol turned it down (saying it was too wild for their repertoire), The Rivingtons (named after Rivington Street in New York City) went to Liberty Records. "The people at Liberty loved it," says Al, "but let it sit around for six months without doing anything with it. So the group decided to make some appearances for the disc jockeys around town and they started playing it. It ended up number one in California and just went on from there."

The Rivingtons still perform and make their home in Las Vegas, Nevada.

Papa-Oom-Mow-Mow Candi Carrot Pie

1 1/2 cups carrots
1 stick butter, room temperature
1 can evaporated milk
2 tsp vanilla extract

3 eggs
1/4 tsp nutmeg
2 cups sugar
9" pie crust, pre-baked

Cook carrots until well done, then put in blender with butter. Add eggs, milk, sugar, nutmeg and vanilla and blend first on low speed and then on high speed until creamy smooth. Pour into pie crust. Bake in oven at 300° for 45 minutes. Let cool 20 minutes and serve.

Jimmie Rodgers

The year 1957 was quite a year for Jimmie Rodgers. He auditioned for *The Arthur Godfrey Talent Scout Show* and won. In July, he recorded a song called "Honeycomb" (his first million seller) and in the same year had another number-one song, "Kisses Sweeter Than Wine." The year 1958 brought "Oh! Oh! I'm Falling In Love Again," "Bim Bom Bay,"

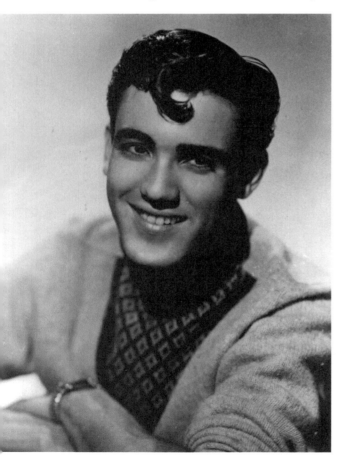

"Secretly" and "Are You Really, Really Mine." From 1957 to 1960, Jimmie appeared in all the major nightclubs in the United States and abroad, and was seen on all of the major TV shows of the day: Ed Sullivan, Perry Como, Dinah Shore, Patti Page and Dick Clark.

In the early '60s, Jimmie went to Hollywood to try his hand at acting. He succeeded in starring in two films, *The Little Shepherd Of Kingdom Come* with George Kennedy and Chill Wills and *Back Door To Hell* with Jack Nicholson.

Then, on the night of December 20, 1967, on his way home from a Christmas party in Los Angeles, Jimmie was stopped by two off-duty police officers and beaten so severely that he was hospitalized with head injuries requiring three brain operations. He also suffered a broken arm and leg injuries. The officers left the scene with Jimmie closer to death than life. His hospital stay lasted over a year and left him requiring extensive rehabilitation treatment. The two policemen involved in the incident were dismissed from the police department, and in 1973 Jimmie settled his legal matter out of court.

Today Jimmie, his wife, Mary Louise, and their family live just a few miles from Brandsen, Missouri, where they all perform. They are dear friends.

Kisses Sweeter Than Wine Cake

1 pkg yellow cake mix
1 1/2 tsp nutmeg
4 eggs
3/4 cup oil
1 large pkg vanilla instant
   pudding
Salt, dash
3/4 cup cream sherry wine

Beat all ingredients together for 5 minutes. Generously oil bundt pan and pour batter into pan. Bake at 350° for 45–50 minutes. Check with toothpick at 45 minutes. Cake is done when it comes out clean. For icing, drizzle 1 1/4 cups powdered sugar thinned with a little sherry on cake while still warm.

Linda Ronstadt

Linda Marie Ronstadt is a national treasure, having recorded 28 albums beginning in 1966 with The Stone Poneys. *Evergreen*, the group's second album, featured Linda singing "Different Drum," which reached number thirteen on the *Billboard* charts.

In 1971, Linda recruited a group of amazing musicians to record her fourth album, including Bernie Leadon, Glenn Frey, Randy Meisner and Don Henley, who later became The Eagles. Four years later, with the help of manager/producer Peter Asher, Linda established what would become a familiar pattern of mixing carefully chosen oldie revivals with new songs. *Heart Like A Wheel* topped the charts and earned Linda her second gold record.

From country, jazz, rock and pop to the Big Band sound—she recorded two albums with Nelson Riddle!—Linda has never been afraid to go where she has never been before, most recently recording three albums in Spanish, the language of her father.

The multi-talented Linda starred in the Broadway production of *The Pirates of Penzance* in 1981, and in the film in 1983. She has received an American Music Award, an Emmy, two Academy of Country Music Awards, and six Grammys (including one with Emmy Lou Harris and Dolly Parton for "Trio" and another with Aaron Neville for "All My Life"). Pretty cool credentials!

"This music gets you through everything," Linda says about the songs on her latest album, *Frenesi*, a seductive collection of Afro-Cuban rhythms. "There is nothing like this on the radio. The culture has not supported these well-crafted songs; we are being robbed of a rich experience from Latin and Black music."

Corn Muffins Ronstadt

1 cup whole wheat-flour
1 cup yellow corn meal,
   whole meal
4 tsp baking powder
1/2 tsp salt (optional)

1/4 cup sugar
2 eggs, lightly beaten
1 cup skim milk
3 Tbsp butter, melted
1 cup cream-style corn

In a large bowl, combine first 5 ingredients. In a medium bowl, combine eggs, milk, butter and corn. Add this to the dry ingredients, stirring until dry ingredients are moistened. Spoon the batter into 12 greased muffin cups. Bake in a preheated oven at 425° for 20–25 minutes or until the tops are golden.

Rosie And The Originals
Rosie Hamlin

Rosie Hamlin grew up in the San Diego area of Southern California. When she was a fifteen-year-old student at Sweetwater High School, she wrote a song that would become a classic—"Angel Baby." Just a few months later, in 1961, Rosie And The Originals were at the top of the charts for over six weeks.

Rosie says, "One of my most memorable experiences was meeting Jackie Wilson. I was fifteen years old and my boyfriend and guitar player, Noah Tafolla, was on a show with about 25 acts at the United Artists Theatre. Jackie was the star and 'Lonely Teardrops' was a huge hit. But he was so nice to us. He introduced us to his manager and they had us fly to New York to record an album for Brunswick. We did some great shows with Jackie back East, and I would always stand in the wings and watch him when he performed. He was such a high energy, dynamic individual. Just dynamite. I don't recall ever seeing anyone dance like he did or have such control over his voice."

Rosie was thrilled when John Lennon recorded "Angel Baby" on his *Menlove Ave* album and was quoted in *Life* magazine saying Rosie was one of his favorite American artists.

Today, Rosie lives in Redlands, California, and continues to write and perform. She's a loving and giving person who helped us out by appearing at the first West Coast show to benefit The National Music Foundation.

Angel Baby's Angel Food Cake

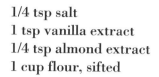

1 1/2 cups sugar
1/2 cup water
1 1/4 cups egg whites
1 tsp cream of tartar

1/4 tsp salt
1 tsp vanilla extract
1/4 tsp almond extract
1 cup flour, sifted

While humming the chorus of "Angel Baby," heat sugar and water to 242° or until syrup spins a long thread. Beat egg whites with salt and continue beating until egg whites hold a peak. Slowly pour syrup over beaten egg whites and continue beating until mixture is cold. Add vanilla and almond extract. Fold in flour. Cut through batter with spatula to remove large air bubbles. Bake in ungreased tube pan in moderate heat (350°) for 45 minutes. Invert pan and let cake hang in pan until cool. Makes one 10" cake. Invite your angel over tonight and serve with candlelight!

The Safaris
Marv Rosenberg

Safari Marv Rosenberg remembers how he came up with the incredible hit song, "Image Of A Girl." "I was dating a girl and stopped by her house one day. She was upset when I arrived and said, 'This is ridiculous. You spend nearly all your time at rehearsals with your group or doing shows somewhere. You don't have any time for me and I can't take this anymore. I need to know right now: Is it me or is it your music?' I was bushed and downcast, and I asked her if I could go lie down on her bed. Well, she had this really loud clock in her room, and there was a drip coming from the bathroom. That formed the beginning and the rest just came to me. I asked her for a piece of paper and a pencil. I wrote the whole thing in about five minutes."

The Safaris were going into the studio to record a song called "4 Steps To Love," which was going to be their first A-side. Marv recalls, "It took us nineteen takes. We had about ten minutes of studio time left and we were told to hurry up and get a B-side done. We ran through 'Image Of A Girl' twice and then recored it. Obviously, 'Image Of A Girl' became the A-side and was the hit of the summer in 1960."

Marv eventually went back to school and received his Ph.D. in psychology, and currently he works out of a hospital in Los Angeles. "But," he says, "my heart will always be in music—especially oldies. That's the music I was brought up with and that's the music I still love." Today, Marv lives in the San Fernando Valley area of Los Angeles. He enjoys performing occasionally as The Safaris with original lead singer Jim Stephens and Buck Buchanan.

Image Of A Swirl (A Marble Cake)

1 3/4 cups cake flour, sifted
2 tsp baking powder
1/2 tsp salt
1/2 cup shortening
1 cup sugar

2 eggs, beaten
1/2 cup milk
1 1/2 tsp vanilla
1 oz (1 square) chocolate
2 Tbsp milk

Sift flour, baking powder and salt together. Cream shortening and sugar until fluffy. Add eggs. Add sifted dry ingredients and 1/2 cup milk, alternating in small amounts and beating well after each addition. Add vanilla. Divide batter in halves. Melt chocolate and add with the 2 Tbsp milk to one half, blending well. Drop batter by tablespoonfuls alternately into greased pan. Bake at 350° for 50–60 minutes. Makes one 8" x 8" cake.

Tommy Sands

Tommy was "discovered" at the age of twelve by none other than Elvis' manager, Colonel Tom Parker. Tommy traveled extensively through the South with Elvis' show and received his first major exposure when, at the suggestion of the Colonel, he substituted for Elvis in the nationally televised NBC special, *The Singing Idol.* The featured song in the program, "Teenage Crush," became a

million seller for Tommy on Capitol Records in just one week. This first hit was followed by other successes: "Goin' Steady," "I'll Be Seeing You," "Sing Boy Sing," "Ring My Phone," "Sinner Man" and "The Old Oaken Bucket."

Tommy's first motion picture was *Sing Boy Sing* for 20th Century Fox. He not only starred in the film with Edmund O'Brien and Nick Adams but also teamed up with Rod McKuen and wrote the score. His other notable films include *Babes In Toyland* with Annette Funicello and Ray Bolger, *The Longest Day* with John Wayne and Richard Burton, *None But The Brave* with Frank Sinatra and Clint Walker, *Mardi Gras* with Pat Boone and *Love In A Goldfish Bowl* with Fabian.

Tommy has performed in over 100 TV dramas and has made countless variety show appearances. He has been nominated for an Emmy Award on five occasions. As a nightclub entertainer, he has played every major club in the United States and is as well known in Europe, Australia, Japan and the Far East as he is here at home. In the late '60s, Tommy moved to Hawaii where, for many years, he drew capacity crowds at the Outrigger Hotel in Waikiki. Today, he makes his home in the San Fernando Valley area of Los Angeles and continues to create and perform.

Pineapple Crush Pie (Not Just For Teenagers)

3/4 cup sugar
1/3 cup flour
1/8 tsp salt
2 cups milk, scalded
1/2 tsp vanilla extract

2 Tbsp butter
2 eggs, well beaten
1 cup crushed pineapple, well drained
1 baked pie shell
Whipped cream

Combine butter, sugar, salt, flour and eggs. Add scalded milk slowly, stirring constantly. Cook in double boiler over hot water until thick and smooth. Add vanilla and pineapple. Heat thoroughly. Pour into baked pie shell. Cool thoroughly at room temperature, then chill in refrigerator for several hours. Serve with whipped cream.

The Shirelles

In 1958, while still attending high school in Passaic, New Jersey, The Shirelles were signed by Tiara Records. Their first single, "I Met Him On A Sunday," was an instant hit. Tiara Records then became Scepter Records, and the girls' second release, "Dedicated To The One I Love," sold over a million copies. This was followed by another million seller, "Tonight's The Night." After these three major hits, Carole King entered their lives, writing and arranging their next single, "Will You Still Love Me Tomorrow," which sold over three million records. Hit followed hit including such classics as "Baby, It's You," "Foolish Little Girl," "Everybody Loves A Lover," "Mama Said," "A Thing Of The Past," "What A Sweet Thing That Was" and their five-million-selling record, "Soldier Boy." The Shirelles soon became known all over the world, and their records became legendary. They were voted the number one Female Vocal Group for five years in a row by *Billboard, Cashbox* and *Record World* magazines.

In 1963, they were asked to record the theme song for the hit movie, *It's A Mad, Mad, Mad, Mad World*. In June 1991, the original Shirelles: Beverly Lee, Shirley Alston Reeves, and Doris Jackson (Micky Harris passed away on June 10, 1982,) reunited to receive The Soul Of American Music Award presented to them by Dionne Warwick.

I Met Him On A Sundae
Beverly Lee

1 scoop black raspberry ice cream
1 scoop chocolate ice cream
2 scoops vanilla ice cream
1 scoop strawberry ice cream
Dash chocolate syrup
Dash marshmallow topping
Fresh sliced strawberries or canned
Fresh pineapples or canned
Top with whipped cream

Decide and design as you wish, and enjoy!

Mama Said Bake Cranberry Bread
Shirley Alston Reeves (formerly of The Shirelles)

1/2 cup Parkay spread or light spread
3/4 cup sugar
2 eggs
3 cups flour
1 Tbsp baking powder
1 tsp salt

1/2 tsp baking soda
1 cup Kraft pure 100% unsweetened
    pasteurized orange juice
1 cup cranberries, coarsely chopped
1/2 cup nuts, chopped

Beat spread and sugar until light and fluffy. Add eggs, 1 at a time, mixing well after each addition. Mix dry ingredients and add juice. Stir in cranberries and nuts. Pour into greased, floured 9" x 5" loaf pan. Bake at 350° for 1 hour 15 minutes or until wooden pick inserted in center comes out clean. Cool 5 minutes, remove from pan. Serve with sweet orange spread. Makes 1 loaf.

The Skyliners

Although their very first recording became a multi-million-selling smash that has been recorded by more than 100 other artists to date, The Skyliners were not an overnight success. In fact, they struggled for over two years before they ever got the opportunity to step into a recording studio, playing anywhere they could get an audience—from out-of-the-way beer taverns to downtown record hops, usually for little or no pay. But the experience paid off when "Since I Don't Have You" (written by lead singer Jimmy Beaumont and the group's first and only manager Joe Rock) became an international hit, and The Skyliners stepped out onto major stages around the world. "Since I Don't Have You" was followed by their other great hits: "This I Swear," "It Happened Today" and "Pennies From Heaven."

Today, The Skyliners celebrate over 30 years of traveling around the world giving great performances and making thousands of friends. "Since I Don't Have You" continues to be recorded by other artists and was recently a huge hit for Ronnie Milsap. Jimmy and the rest of the group still reside in Pittsburgh and continue to be managed by Joe Rock. We worked with them at the Greek Theatre in Los Angeles in 1989 and not only were they really fantastic performers but also incredibly nice people.

Since I Don't Have Shoo-fly Pie

1/4 cup shortening
1 1/2 cups flour
1 cup brown sugar
3/4 tsp baking soda
1/4 tsp salt
3/4 cup molasses

3/4 cup hot water
1/8 tsp nutmeg
Cinnamon, pinch
Ginger
Cloves
Unbaked pie shell

For the crumb part, work together shortening, flour and brown sugar. Set aside. For the liquid part, thoroughly mix the baking soda, salt, molasses, nutmeg, cinnamon, ginger and cloves, then add hot water. Into an unbaked pie shell, alternately layer the crumbs and liquid, with crumbs on bottom and top. Bake 15 minutes at 450°, then 20 minutes at 350°.

The Teddy Bears
Carol Connors

Carol Connors was born and raised in Los Angeles. "I was weaned on opera," she recalls. "I was singing *'La donna é mobile'* before I learned 'Row, Row, Row Your Boat.'" While still in high school, Carol's career was launched with a ten-dollar loan from her parents. The money went toward making a demo of a song her classmate, Phil Spector, had written called "To Know Him Is To Love Him." Phil loved Carol's voice, and she became the lead singer for The Teddy Bears. The other two members of the group were Phil Spector and Marshall Leib.

That ten-dollar investment may have been one of the best in show business. A few months later, The Teddy Bears' record had sold nearly three million copies and was to earn spot number 76 on *Billboard*'s list of the Top 200 singles of the last twenty years.

After The Teddy Bears disbanded, Carol went on to become a very successful songwriter. She enjoyed the distinction of being the only woman to have written a mega-hit in the ultra-macho genre of hot-rod songs. "Hey Little Cobra" was—and remains—an American car-song classic.

But it was another macho property that put Carol on the map. She co-wrote the lyrics for "Gonna Fly Now" (Bill Conti wrote the music), the theme for the Academy Award winner, *Rocky*. She has also written songs for films such as *The Earthling, Looking For Mr. Goodbar,* and Walt Disney's *The Rescuers*, and has penned special music for TV's *Days Of Our Lives* and *Lifestyles Of The Rich And Famous* (including the show's theme, "Champagne Wishes And Cavier Dreams"). Carol lives in Beverly Hills, California.

Auntie Carol's You Can Hardly Bear It Carat Cake (Rocky Loves It!)

2 cups sugar
2 cups flour
2 tsp baking soda
2 tsp baking powder
1/2 tsp salt
4 eggs
1 cup oil, Wesson or Mazola

3 cups raw carrots, finely grated
1/4 cup nuts

Mix ingredients by hand—do not use mixer—then add carrots and nuts. (If desired add raisins, coconut and pineapple in amounts to satisfy taste buds)
Bake in 9" x 13" pan for 1 hour at 350°.

Auntie Carol's Dreamy Creamy Frosting

4 oz cream cheese
1/4 cup butter
1 3/4 cups powdered sugar
1 tsp vanilla
(Also add raisins, coconut and pineapple, if desired, for those taste buds)

Beat all ingredients by hand or mixer until creamy.

Stevie Wonder

Accepting awards has always been a part of Stevie's career. One of the world's most vocal opponents of apartheid, Stevie accepted his Oscar for the movie *The Woman In Red* in the name of Nelson Mandela, which promptly resulted in the banning of his music in South Africa.

Born on May 13th in Saginaw, Michigan, Stevie was the third of six children. Blind since birth, he never looked upon his blindness as a handicap. He played games, rode his bike and climbed trees just like his childhood friends.

Stevie came to Motown as Steveland Judkins in 1961 after Ronnie White of The Miracles introduced the young singer to Berry Gordy. Impressed by Stevie's tremendous untapped talent, the company changed his name to Little Stevie Wonder. His first number-one record, "Fingertips II," was recorded in 1963 and launched an enduring international career in music. It was followed by such singles as "Uptight, Everything Is Alright," "My Cherie Amour" and " For Once In My Life."

When Stevie turned 21, he decided to take more creative control of his music. He proceeded to display his superior ability to produce by engineering three albums that would receive Album-of-the-Year Grammys. He further demonstrated his production talents during the '80s with his Oscar-nominated score for *The Secret Life Of Planets* and Oscar-winning song "I Just Called to Say I Love You"

from *The Woman in Red*. He has won a total of fourteen Grammys and an Award Of Merit at the American Music Awards for his achievements in the music industry.

Stevie Wonder can be listed as world-renowned singer/songwriter, producer and humanitarian, but the title he loves most is "Father." Quality time is always spent with his daughter, Aisha, and his sons, Keita and Mumtaz.

Do I Do Oatmeal Cookies

1 cup shortening
1 cup brown sugar
2 eggs
1 tsp vanilla
1 1/2 cups flour

1 tsp salt
1 tsp soda
3 cups oatmeal
1 cup nuts, chopped
1 cup raisins

Cream shortening and sugar. Add eggs and vanilla. Beat well. Sift together-flour, salt and soda and add to creamed mixture. Stir in oats, nuts and raisins. Mix. Drop by teaspoons onto an ungreased cookie sheet. Bake at 350° for 10 minutes or until lightly browned.

The Collector's Page

DINAH
WASHINGTON

For information on how to order this Rock 'n' Roll/ Rhythm and Blues Commemorative Stamp, please see page 2.

Breakfasts and Midnight Snacks

Tunafish Malted

Pamela's Morning-After Aphrodisiac Brew-Ha-Ha

Chocolava Stump Logs

The Wanderer's Trail Mix

Mr. Postman Toasties

Iggy's Breakfast (Any Stooge Can Make It)

Jam Up and Jelly Tight

Pocket Full Of Banana Pancakes

Alice Cooper

Being described as "a legend in their own time" is certainly a cliché, but nobody in Rock & Roll has taken such a vivid imagination and madcap persona to the people with as much controversy and success as has Alice Cooper.

The Master of Shock-rock, Alice has been a disturbing proposition from the very beginning. Debuting in 1970, he soon turned the music world inside out— wearing outrageous get-ups and drippy make-up, and performing his twisted laments through a busted-out window frame.

"We were into fun, sex, death and money when everybody else was into peace and love," Alice explains. "We drove a stake through the heart of the love generation."

Alice Cooper shook up the minds of teenagers all around the world, bringing him countless gold and platinum albums featuring such rebellious anthems as "18," "Elected" and "No More Mr. Nice Guy," as well as the classic, "Only Women Bleed."

Alice made his greatest impact on stage, utilizing multi-level stage sets and elaborate scenery in ways unprecedented for a rock act. Audiences gasped and cheered over such props as a guillotine, an electric chair and gallows, with Alice usually portraying the victim.

Alice Cooper brought show biz and Rock & Roll together in ways never seen before or since, and it's no surprise that after all the shock waves he created, the legend of Alice Cooper continues strong in the '90s.

Although Alice is now clean and sober, his alcohol escapades are legendary in the annals of Rock & Roll. He'll still go you shot- for-shot, but with ginger ale please.

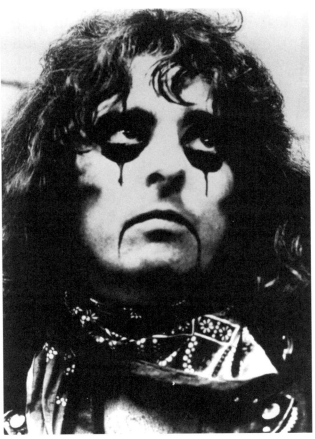

Tunafish Malted (For Hangovers)

1 can tuna fish
2 scoops pistachio ice cream
4 oz cream

Blend. Drink. Go back to bed.

GTOs
PAMELA DES BARRES

In 1969, Pamela Des Barres, along with her hysterical gang of unique girl-friends, known as The GTO's (Girls Together Outrageously), released an album on Bizarre Records called *Permanent Damage*, inspired and produced by Frank Zappa. The GTO's were one of the most notorious all-girl bands around, and because they didn't play instruments, they were backed up on their record and at gigs by an amazing array of musicians. Jeff Beck played lead on a couple tracks, and if you listen closely you can hear Rod Stewart singing back-up vocals on "Mercy's Tune." One outrageous night at a Hollywood nightclub called Thee Experience, John Bonham from Zeppelin played drums as the girls frolicked around the stage, with Noel Redding (Jimi Hendrix Experience) on bass! The GTOs were an infamous part of the Rock & Roll '60s, making heads and minds turn whenever they entered a room.

Many years later, Pamela dug out all of her old faithful diaries and wrote a best-selling book about her rocky, romantic relationships with rock's heroes and the magic of the free-love '60s called *I'm With the Band: Confessions of a*

Groupie, followed by the sequel, *Take Another Little Piece of My Heart: A Groupie Grows Up*. Pamela, who has been called "the avatar of post-feminist life-writers," has become an oddball spokesperson for her high-flying generation, turning up on all the talk shows—from *Donahue* to *Oprah*—defending female sexuality and proclaiming the ecstasy of Rock & Roll.

Pamela's Morning-After Aphrodisiac Brew-Ha-Ha (For Two)

1 mango, chopped
1 handful strawberries, fresh or frozen
1 peach or nectarine, chopped

1 full glass fresh orange juice
1 cup lemon low-fat yogurt
A couple drops of vanilla

Whip up all this yummy stuff in the blender on high speed with a few ice cubes and find yourself back in ecstasy.

Devo
Mark Mothersbaugh

Devo, formed in 1972 in Akron, Ohio, spouted an original, tongue-in-cheek world view, announcing that man was in a state of genetic and cultural "devolution." "All we're doing is reporting the facts," said vocalist Mark Mothersbaugh. "Devolution is basically an extended joke that is as valid an explanation as anything in the Bible is, a mythology for people to believe in. We were just attacking the ideas that people have that they must be the center of the universe." The details of the group's pre-Devo existence have been intentionally obscured as part of their automaton image, but we know that Mark Mothersbaugh and Jerry Casale met while studying art at Kent State University. Along with Bob I (Mothersbaugh) and Bob II (Casale), the two artists produced a ten-minute video, "The Truth About Devolution." The video won a prize at the Ann Arbor Film Festival, and the band started playing club dates.

In 1976, their first single, "Jocko Homo," was released on their own Boogie Boy Records, and one year later the follow-up, a syncopated version of the Rolling Stones' "Satisfaction," increased the band's growing cult.

Devo converted Iggy Pop, who included their "Praying Hands" in his act. Iggy brought them to the attention of other artists in the forefront of rock exploration—David Bowie and Brian Eno, who produced *Q: Are We Not Men? A: We Are Devo!* in the fall of 1978.

Devo's third album, *Freedom of Choice*, included the manic "Whip It," which stirred up audiences across America, and became a million seller. Several ersatz hit covers followed, including Johnny Rivers' "Secret Agent Man" and Lee Dorsey's "Working in a Coal Mine."

Mark Mothersbaugh, who gave us this magnificent recipe, now scores feature films and TV projects, creates music/sound design for interactive software, and continues to show his visual artwork internationally.

Chocolava Stump Logs

1 12-pack order of Pioneer Chicken Carry-out Logs
1 can Bosco chocolate sauce

Place room temperature sauce into bowl, then carefully dip chicken logs into sauce (chicken nuggets can be substituted in an emergency). Arrange on plate in either Lincoln Log cabin or smiley face shapes. Enjoy!

Specify free-range chicken and pesticide-free chocolate syrup.

Dion

The mastery of Dion DiMucci began at a very early age on the mean streets of the Bronx in New York. Dion was born into a show-business family. His father, a professional puppeteer, would often take him on summer tours, but it was in the bars and on the street corners of his Bronx neighborhood that Dion's musical apprenticeship really began. R & B, blues, doo-wop, Tin Pan Alley and early Rock & Roll all influenced him. But, paradoxically, Country & Western legend Hank Williams was the first to really spark Dion's singing ambitions. Williams' high, lonesome sound attracted Dion, the city boy, who by age twelve had collected hundreds of Hank's singles and could sing them all by heart.

In 1957, Dion brought the best of the neighborhood crooners together to form the group Dion and The Belmonts—named after Belmont Avenue in the heart of the Bronx. "I Wonder Why" was Dion's first hit with The Belmonts. With songs such as "A Teenager In Love" and "Where Or When," the group earned their place in the history books. Then, venturing out as a solo artist in 1960, Dion racked up a string of number-one hits that many still consider to be the best songs of that or any other era: "Lonely Teenager," "Runaround Sue," "The Wanderer," "Lovers Who Wander," "Love Came To Me," "Ruby Baby," "Donna The Prima Donna" and the moving "Abraham, Martin And John."

Today, Dion has just completed a new album, *Yo Frankie*, for Arista Records. An autobiographical book titled *The Wanderer* was published by William Morrow, and a recent induction into the Rock & Roll Hall Of Fame highlighted Dion's contribution to the music industry.

The Wanderer's Trail Mix

1/2 cup pumpkin seeds, shelled
1/2 cup almonds
1/2 cup cashews, raw
1/2 cup coconut, shredded

1/2 cup raisins
1/2 cup dried apricots
1/2 cup pineapple, dried and diced
1 cup dried apple slices

Mix it up and you can hit the road!

The Marvelettes
Gladys Horton

In 1961, Gladys Horton, Katherine Anderson and Wanda Young were attending high school in Detroit when they decided to sing in a local talent show. There they were discovered by Berry Gordy, Jr., who promptly signed them to Tamla Records. With Miss Horton's sassy lead vocal on "Please Mr. Postman," The Marvelettes catapulted to the top of the charts—just shortly after Gladys' fifteenth birthday!

Gladys then wrote a song called "Playboy." Again, with her unique voice singing the lead, The Marvelettes had another smash hit. Eight years and many hit records later—including Motown's first number-one hit—Gladys retired from performing to become a full-time mom.

Fortunately, she's kept her famous vocal chords in top form, and today Gladys and her Marvelettes are back, traveling throughout the United States and Europe. Their songs set the stage for an era in music history that is truly unforgettable.

In 1962, we performed with The Marvelettes at the Cow Palace in San Francisco and they tore the place down! They were—and still are—fantastic.

Mr. Postman Toasties

2 or more slices wheat bread
Raisins
Margarine

Pre-heat oven or toaster oven to 400°. Place 2 or more slices of wheat bread on a lightly greased cookie sheet. Spread margarine and sprinkle raisins on bread. For variety, add 2 or 3 slices of peaches or apples topped with cinnamon, or orange slices sprinkled with pecans or walnut bits. Cook in oven for 2–3 minutes. Do not overcook or burn.

Iggy Pop

O.K. I'm Iggy Pop + this is my life. I got born in Michigan, 1947, Mom + Dad hardworking + arrow-straight. Schoolteacher + executive secretary. Lived at Coachville Garden Mobile Home Court, Lot 96, 3423 Carpenter Rd., Ypsilanti, Michigan U.S.A. Age 5 played drums with my Lincoln Logs + Tinkertoys. Age 8 heard Sinatra, wanted to sing. Smart in school, but no homework. Most likely to succeed, 9th grade. 10th grade, 1962 formed Iguanas, high school rock band. We cut a single our senior year, and the summer of 1965 we got a gig in northern Michigan at a joint called the Ponytail Club. Wow! Professional employment, far away from home. Five 45-minute sets a night, 15-minute breaks, 6 nights a week, a bare cabin with cold running water and one electric socket. Pay – 50 bucks a week. I plugged a phonograph into that socket and listened to "Out Of Our Heads" and "Bringing It All Back Home" all summer. Started getting wild, grew my hair to my shoulders + dyed it platinum. Got arrested + took my first mug shot. Got fired from Ponytail. U of Michigan, dropped out '66. Blues band called Prime Movers, playing bars, Detroit + Chicago sometimes.

Love Butterfield Band/Junior Wells/Buddy Guy/Little Walter/Otis Rush/Wow.

Found 2 high-school dropouts on Michigan street-corner, '67, to start Stooges. Totally did our own thing, like nobody else. 3 great albums '69, '70, '73. Went nuts from the life, got screwed in the business and went to L.A., went underground, more arrests, hard times. Resurfaced '76 with 1st solo album, recorded by Bowie. Lived in Europe with Bowie 2 years, 2 albums, both great. 1 live recording, so-so.

Loved Berlin, hated L.A. Still do. Both. Lots more albums (total 15) half great, half so-so, ups, downs, N.Y.C., London, N.Y.C. again, permanent headquarters now, got a place in Mexico to go when I can't stand it anymore, love my garden, my dog + cat, a lot; but also love noise, aggravation, girls, regular guys, music, as such. Drink beer + wine sometimes, hate publicity whores, hokey music, people who wanna use me, + conceited dicks. Ambition is to make better music, live life in peace, + then die. Check out my f***ing record because its really good. When i play around your town check that out too, becuz that'll be the same, only more.

(Iggy Pop, N.Y.C., '93)

Iggy's Breakfast
(Any Stooge Can Make It)

Make a cup of black coffee. Take 1 croissant and put it in the toaster oven at 400° until brown. Remove the croissant. (Don't forget to turn off the toaster oven!) Dunk the croissant into the black coffee and SLURP!

Tommy Roe

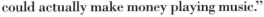

Atlanta-born singer/songwriter Tommy Roe took up the guitar when he was thirteen and began composing about the same time. In high school he formed a band, The Satimes, which soon became a very popular act around the South, circa 1960. "We were just doing it for the fun of performing," Tommy recalls. "But the gigs got better and better. And I suddenly realized, at that tender age, that you could actually make money playing music."

So, in 1962, Tommy signed a contract with ABC Records and released a song that he had written, called "Sheila." This began a string of tremendous successes throughout the decade that included "Everybody," "Sweet Pea," "Hooray For Hazel," "Dizzy" and "Jam Up And Jelly Tight."

Today, Tommy lives in Atlanta and Beverly Hills. He has continued both to perform in concerts and shows throughout the years and to write his own music. He says, "I have a much better handle on who I am now and what I'm doing than ever before. My music pleases me—and that's important, because in the past I always tried too hard to please everyone else."

Tommy is always fun to work with. We've done a number of shows with him during the past five years. He was also one of the giving people who not long ago helped us put on a benefit show for The National Music Foundation on the West Coast.

Jam Up And Jelly Tight
(A Grilled Peanut Butter 'N Jelly Snack That'll Make You Dizzy)

2 slices white bread, crusts removed

2 Tbsp peanut butter

2 Tbsp grape jelly (you can use another flavor, but grape is my favorite)

2 tsp powdered sugar

2 Tbsp butter, soft

After trimming off bread crusts, put peanut butter on one piece and grape jelly on the other. Put together. Butter both of the outer sides of the bread with the soft butter. Grill (like a grilled cheese sandwich) until both sides are golden brown. Remove from skillet and put on plate. Sprinkle with powdered sugar. Serve when warm, but not hot, right after cooking.

The Spin Doctors
Chris Barron

The swell new band, The Spin Doctors, was put together three years ago at New York's now legendary New School of Jazz. Savvy, spiritual and sexy, the Doctors' music makes you want to dance hard, laugh a lot and put on your thinking cap.

"We're the last flight of the quill before the keyboard and console take over," quips the poet-laureate singer/ songwriter Chris Barron. "Our sound just kind of revealed itself to us," adds guitarist Eric Schenkman, "like some kind of crazy sandwich where strange things happen and two plus two equals five."

On a recent four-month blitz of the States, which looped around 50,000 miles of coastal and heartland highway, the Doctors continued to win new converts and woo the rock world. About their first album, *Pocket Full Of Kryptonite*, Eric says "This album stinks of Bleecker Street at five in the morning. This is a real Manhattan album; even the sweet songs have grit." Packed with real-rock hits that created a nationwide network of dance-crazed Spinheads at live shows, the album has produced three solid singles—"Jimmy Olsen's Blues," "Two Princes" and the infectious "Little Miss Can't Be Wrong." A tribute to The Spin Doctors' lasting appeal and long-term placement on the charts is the fact that both musicians and the general public love this burning, bouncy band.

Pocket Full Of Banana Pancakes

1 part mashed bananas
  (the riper, the better)
1 part pancake mix
1 part milk (soy milk works, too)
Lots of good chocolate
Nuts, if you like (walnuts are good)

An egg, 1 for a small batch,
  2 for a big one
Honey, cinnamon, vanilla or almond
  extract, or bits of ripe pear (or whatever else is yummy or just around) can
  be added

Place mix in a bowl and shape like a volcano. In something else, beat the egg really well and add it to the mix. Add everything else to the mix. Stir very, very gently (rough mixing makes tough pancakes). Heat griddle until things sizzle on it. Fry up pancakes on the griddle.

Artist Index

Food Index

Photo Credits

The following photos are courtesy of MICHAEL OCHS ARCHIVES/Venice, CA: 4, 5, 12, 14, 16, 18, 20, 22, 24, 28, 32, 34, 36, 38, 40, 44, 46, 48, 52, 54, 56, 58, 60, 62, 66, 70, 76, 78, 80, 84, 90, 91 (BMI PHOTO ARCHIVES/MOA), 92, 100, 102, 104, 107, 108, 110, 112, 114, 116, 118, 120, 122, 124, 126, 130, 132, 134, 136, 138, 140, 142, 144, 146, 150, 152, 154, 156, 158, 160, 164, 166, 168, 170, 174, 176, 182, 184 (BMI PHOTO ARCHIVES/MOA), 186, 188, 190, 192, 194, 196, 198, 202, 206, 208, 210, 212, 214, 216, 218, 220, 222, 228, 230, 233 (top), and 234

26, 27: Michael Lavine, 1992
50, 51: Chris Cuffaro
53: Dennis Keeley
57: Dave Harmon
65: John Ragel, 9/92
72, 73: Albert Sanchez
74: Lance Mercer
75: Chris Cuffaro
86, top: Peggy Sirota; bottom right: Eric Watson
88, 89: Michael Miller
94: Daniel Corrigan, 1987
95: Per Breifhagen
96, 97: Henry Diltz

117: Gene Martin
148, 149: Annie Leibowitz
167: Alan Clark
172-173: Baron Wolman
178: David Jenson
179: Robert Molnar
181: Larry Williams
193: Tom Bert, 1987
205: Robert Blakeman, 1989
215: Guy Calabro Photo
217: Alan Degan
223: Randee St. Nicholas
224: Baron Wolman
227: Jonathan Gelber, 1988
233 (bottom): Michael Lavine
236, 237: Paul La Raia